I0128949

'The notion of creativity in the arts and creative industries remains poorly analyzed and fraught with unproven assumptions about gender and artistic temperament. O'Driscoll's analysis of the concept of creativity is matched with her valuable interviews with women in diverse areas of artistic practice, persuasively countering the presumption that women possess inferior creative capacities'.

Carolyn Korsmeyer, author of *Gender and Aesthetics: An Introduction*

Creative Women in Ireland

Through the contributions of women working in the creative industries, this timely book explores the role of creativity in their lives, the experiences that have positively contributed to and supported their creativity and their work, as well as how gendered considerations intersect with their involvement in the cultural sphere.

Spanning psychology, cultural and media studies, and the philosophy of art, it builds on existing research by offering examples of the abundance of creativity residing in women working in film and television, architecture, design, music, theatre, and the performing and visual arts in Ireland. Their reflections offer a valuable counter perspective to the assumption that women are more naturally the 'muse' than the creator. From these conversations, some common, although at times diverging, experiences in childhood and early career and approaches to their creative work offer important insights into the nature and practice of creativity and the conditions that may best nurture and support creativity in girls and women.

Providing original observations into gendered understandings of creativity, this book will be essential reading for researchers, advanced students, and practitioners seeking contemporary insights on creativity, feminism, and gender.

Dr Aileen O'Driscoll is Assistant Professor in Media and Communications at the School of Communications, Dublin City University. Her current research interests include the Creative and Cultural Industries; Women's Studies and feminist theory; and the involvement, role and representation of women in the media industries.

Routledge Focus on the Global Creative Economy
Series Editor: Aleksandar Brkić, *Goldsmiths, University of London, UK*

This innovative Shortform book series aims to provoke and inspire new ways of thinking, new interpretations, emerging research, and insights from different fields. In rethinking the relationship of creative economies and societies beyond the traditional frameworks, the series is intentionally inclusive. Featuring diverse voices from around the world, books in the series bridge scholarship and practice across arts and cultural management, the creative industries and the global creative economy.

Innovation in the Arts
Concepts, Theories, and Practices
Jason C. White

Creative Women in Ireland
Not Your Muse
Aileen O'Driscoll

For more information about this series, please visit: www.routledge.com /Routledge-Focus-on-the-Global-Creative-Economy/book-series/RFGCE

Creative Women in Ireland

Not Your Muse

Aileen O'Driscoll

R Routledge
Taylor & Francis Group

LONDON AND NEW YORK

First published 2023
by Routledge
4 Park Square, Milton Park, Abingdon, Oxon OX14 4RN

and by Routledge
605 Third Avenue, New York, NY 10158

Routledge is an imprint of the Taylor & Francis Group, an informa business

© 2023 Aileen O'Driscoll

The right of Aileen O'Driscoll to be identified as author of this work has been asserted in accordance with sections 77 and 78 of the Copyright, Designs and Patents Act 1988.

All rights reserved. No part of this book may be reprinted or reproduced or utilised in any form or by any electronic, mechanical, or other means, now known or hereafter invented, including photocopying and recording, or in any information storage or retrieval system, without permission in writing from the publishers.

Trademark notice: Product or corporate names may be trademarks or registered trademarks, and are used only for identification and explanation without intent to infringe.

British Library Cataloguing-in-Publication Data
A catalogue record for this book is available from the British Library

Library of Congress Cataloging-in-Publication Data
Names: O'Driscoll, Aileen, author.
Title: Creative women in Ireland: not your muse/Aileen O'Driscoll.
Description: 1 Edition. | New York, NY: Routledge, 2023. |
Series: Routledge focus on the global creative economy |
Includes bibliographical references and index.
Identifiers: LCCN 2022032657 (print) | LCCN 2022032658 (ebook) |
ISBN 9780367534486 (hardback) | ISBN 9780367536565 (paperback) |
ISBN 9781003082750 (ebook)
Subjects: LCSH: Creative ability in women–Ireland. |
Cultural industries–Ireland. | Women–Psychology.
Classification: LCC BF411 .O37 2023 (print) | LCC BF411 (ebook) |
DDC 153.3/509415–dc23/eng/20220824
LC record available at https://lccn.loc.gov/2022032657
LC ebook record available at https://lccn.loc.gov/2022032658

ISBN: 978-0-367-53448-6 (hbk)
ISBN: 978-0-367-53656-5 (pbk)
ISBN: 978-1-003-08275-0 (ebk)

DOI: 10.4324/9781003082750

Typeset in Times New Roman
by Deanta Global Publishing Services, Chennai, India

Contents

Acknowledgements

A sincere thank you to the women who generously gave their time to chat with me for this book. By name: Amanda Coogan: performance art; Annie West: illustration; Carole Pollard: architecture; Jess Kavanagh: music; Lelia Doolan: TV (and, later on, film); Lisa Mulcahy: film; Liz O'Kane: sculpture; Marina Carr: playwright; Oonagh Kearney: film (and formerly theatre); Una Healy: graphic design.

1 Introduction

Examining the intersection of gender and creativity

The celebrated 20th-century poet Robert Graves proclaimed that 'Woman is not a poet; she is either a Muse or she is nothing'. As recently as 2013, renowned German artist George Baselitz was similarly adamant: 'Women don't paint very well. It's a fact'. Stretching back to the ancient Greeks, notions of the artist as referring almost exclusively to men meant that where women were connected to creativity, they usually took the form of muses in being simply considered the sometime source of inspiration for male creators. Gendered understandings of creativity, therefore, have long assumed it to be an innately male trait. But is this preconception still in place and is there evidence for this? Additionally, how do women fare in creative fields and the so-called creative and cultural industries? And for those women who live creative lives, what does creativity mean to them and how might their upbringing have played a role in nurturing their nascent creativity as children? This book takes a look at all of these issues and draws on a range of scholarship to explore such questions. Of central importance, the issue of women's creative involvement in the creative and cultural industries (CCIs) clearly needs careful scrutiny. Indeed, while more attention is now being paid to the issue of women, creativity, and creative labour in the CCIs (Windels and Lee, 2012; Windels and Mallia, 2015; Hesmondhalgh and Baker, 2015; Conor, Gill, and Taylor, 2015; Grow and Deng, 2015), such studies are typically concerned with the realities of being female and creative and how the nexus of those categories has historically been and continues to be defined by tensions and challenges for women who choose to make a living through creative practice.

While clearly it is crucial to document social, structural, and cultural barriers for women, such analyses tend not to offer an insight into the rich inner lives of creative women, although notable and invaluable exceptions include studies by Helson (1965, 1966, 1999) and Reis (2002), among others. This book therefore was interested in capturing, through interviews with a cross-generational cohort of ten creative Irish women[1] involved in a

DOI: 10.4324/9781003082750-1

range of creative practices and industries, their creative outlets as girls and teenagers, whether encouragement and mentorship were present or important, how their careers developed, and what challenges, if any, they have faced. By centring these women's creativity and creative interests, this work aims to be another nail in the coffin of the long-standing trope of the artist and the creative as prototypically male, with woman simply his 'muse'.

Background to the CCIs and considering women's involvement

Academic reference to the 'culture industry' is almost 80 years old and can be dated back to the theories put forward by the critical cultural studies scholars Horkheimer and Adorno, who, in the 1940s, sought to explain how cultural production and art had been 'hijacked' by market forces with the effect of creating cultural texts characterised by their commodified and homogenised essence. In the decades since, discussion and understanding of the cultural and creative industries have moved beyond a solely Marxist, political economy understanding and critique and today incorporates multiple considerations, from cultural studies to sociology and to economic concerns. Indeed, the increasing economic importance of the 'cultural industries', as they came to be referred to from the 1970s and 1980s onwards and later as the 'creative industries' in the 1990s, saw much attention paid by successive governments and policy-makers to this sector of the economy (Hesmondhalgh and Baker, 2011). In particular, UK academics and government documents were very focused, by the late 1990s, on mapping the creative sector. Gross (2020) suggests that, with the publication of the 1998 *Creative Industries Mapping Document*, the UK government under Tony Blair was signalling the seriousness with which it viewed the economic potential of cultural production and it marked the beginning of a concerted effort to systematically categorise the industries that could be considered 'creative' and/or 'cultural'. A subsequent 2001 iteration of this 1998 mapping document would define the creative and cultural industries (the CCIs) as those sectors for which the aspect of creativity and the autonomy and talent of the creative worker to produce something original is at its heart, as is the 'potential for wealth and job creation' (DCMS, 2001, p.5; cited in Henry, 2009, p.143).

Given this broad definition of the sector, policy documents – and, later, scholars and academics – came to consider everything from advertising, design (fashion and graphic), film, television, video, radio, and photography, as well as performing, music, and visual arts, among others, as falling within the umbrella designation of the CCIs. Such an expansive understanding of creative work means that the experience for creative workers spans one of working for large, established, and structured organisations to smaller companies and start-ups, as well as the reality of many creative workers being self-employed and involved in the small-scale 'cottage industry' sector. As such, the CCIs include a disproportionate number of 'solo businesses without employees' and 'large numbers of micro enterprises, freelancers and design manufacturers' (Henry, 2009, p.146). From the Irish perspective, those involved in creative work number far fewer than in the UK. Ireland is also further behind in terms of defining and categorising the sector here. Oliveira (2018) points out that the Irish government's policy documents on this subject are marked by 'confusion' (p.22), while '(s)ome documents present overlapping or contradictory conceptualisations and lack clarity as to which Government department is responsible, as well as guidelines on how to achieve established goals' (Oliveira, 2018, p.22). Further, as noted by Crowley (2017), while there is clear evidence of extensive growth in the CCIs across the EU, 'very little is known about the innovative potential of the creative sector in Ireland' (para.9). In other words, the world of creative and cultural work in Ireland is a nascent and developing one and is, heretofore, underexplored.

In recent years, the focus has shifted away from an exclusive discussion on the financial aspects to instead include a consideration of the nature of the work for those involved in the CCIs. Hesmondhalgh and Baker (2011) note that there is increasing emphasis on the potential for 'greater fulfilment and self-actualisation' (p.5) for creative workers than for workers in other sectors. A crucial factor in this is the ability for many involved in cultural and creative work to set their own schedules and to, in theory, better balance their home lives with the demands of their creative careers. This may suit those people who are drawn to creative work whose personalities may be characterised as 'entrepreneurial' as well as possessing traits associated with 'inspiration, creativity, innovation … self-reliance, autonomy, flexibility and adaptability' (Henry, 2009, p.150). However, out of such assumptions about the prototypical creative worker, scholarship in this field has more recently sought to drill into the experiences of those in a range sectors and from a variety of backgrounds tracked through sex, social class, age, race, ethnicity, sexual orientation, and disability. These studies are interested in 'contextualis(ing) cultural workers in terms of broader social understandings of inequality' (Taylor and O'Brien, 2017, p.2) and in foregrounding issues related to representation, visibility, and career advancement, as well as remuneration, drop-out, and harassment.

While Henry (2009) has lamented the relative dearth of data tracking the picture for women in the CCIs, there has since been some progress made in terms of carrying out empirical research that seeks to document women's involvement in creative and cultural work. For instance, in offering critiques of inaccurate narratives of the CCIs as characterised by equality and diversity, Conor, Gill and Taylor (2015) instead point out that, on the issue of the sexes, 'women as a group are consistently faring worse than men. This is true in advertising, the arts, architecture, computer games development, design, film, radio and television' (p.6). A study published by the European Parliament (McCracken et al., 2018) cites research by the UK which finds that 'women are a minority in virtually every segment of the media sector in the UK, including mainstream news and television, creative industries, gaming, and other digital media industries' (p.18). And, crucially, for those women who are involved in the media industries, they tend to drop out as they get older resulting in the fact that those women who 'survive', as it were, are typically without children and the caring responsibilities associated with motherhood – something that, the report points out, does not appear to impede men in these industries who are fathers.

More recently, significant attention is being paid to women in the film industry, and the figures are stark. In the decade between 2007 and 2017, female directors accounted for a paltry 4% of the top 1,100 films in the US (Liddy, 2020). Of critical importance is the data which indicates that when women are in the director role, 'greater percentages of women were hired as writers, editors, cinematographers and composers compared with films with exclusively male directors' (Liddy, 2020, p.3). Milestone (2015) notes that, more broadly, women across a range of sectors in the CCIs are consistently far outnumbered by male peers in creative roles. She suggests that there are too few ways in which cultures around the globe instil in girls the confidence and the sense of entitlement to be involved in creating our cultural texts. But is the aspect of creative competence and the fact of fewer girls and women exceling in creative spheres relative to boys and men down to simply one of 'you can't be what you can't see?' Or is there something in our biological make-up that explains such discrepancies? The scholarship and studies attempting to define creativity and what traits may best lend themselves to artistic practice shed some light on such questions and debates.

Defining creativity and artistic personalities

The way that creativity has been understood and conceptualised has typically differed between the East and West. From an Eastern perspective, the source of creativity is generally located outside the individual within the sphere of the universe and as such, in order to enhance one's creativity, an appreciation of one's relationship to others, to nature, and to tradition and the past is considered vital (Niu and Sternberg, 2006). Some Western philosophers similarly put forward spiritual and religious theories to posit that creativity manifests through people as an expression of the Divine or by 'the will of the gods' (ibid., p.21). Indeed, 'Plato insisted that great works of poets are entirely inventions of divine Muses ... Poets, therefore, bear only limited responsibility for their work' (ibid.). As a legacy of the Enlightenment period and its emphasis on the secularisation of society and centring of the individual and its associated concepts of free will, autonomy, and agency, creativity in the West thereafter was broadly understood as an talent or trait that could be credited to the person creating literature, poetry, and works of art. This conceptualisation almost entirely supplanted earlier definitions which had relied on spiritual and divine explanations so that creativity came to be associated with the ability of people to bring the aspects of originality and novelty to particular tasks (Lubart and Guignard, 2004). Along with this centring of the individual at the heart of theories of creativity, scholars sought to explore whether certain personalities and traits might be more often in evidence in highly creative people. The field of psychology, in particular, was interested in a 'person-centred perspective' (Rudowicz, 2003, p.274), which looked at 'cognitive factors and personal characteristics, such as motivation, personality, values, problem solving and problem finding orientation' (ibid.) in explaining the creative process. As Rudowicz (2003) explains, studies in this domain tended to identify attributes such as curiosity, confidence, determination, imagination, and non-conformity as often present in creative individuals.

The aspect of non-conformity, or open-mindedness, is one that Schweizer (2006) similarly argues goes hand-in-hand with creativity. The person exhibiting 'openness' typically rejects sex-stereotypical roles and behaviours. This finding that creative people often eschew gendered norms echoes Virginia Woolf's (1929) ideas about the importance of 'psychological androgyny' to the creative mind. In other words, the individual who incorporates qualities commonly associated with both sexes has a greater set of resources to call on, something that aids creativity. Kaufman and Baer (2004) would later also occupy themselves with this question of the creative 'type', with Hesmondhalgh and Baker (2011) noting that psychological theories of creativity and the creative individual were of great interest to the early practitioners of human relations management in the 1950s, who drew on such scholarship in order to try to devise strategies that would get the best out of their workforce. Indeed, the buzz around the concept of 'creativity' and its role in the workplace has not diminished. It continues to be applied across a broad range of industries, but in the CCIs especially, '(c)reative work retains some of its elite associations as positive and special; it is understood to offer the possibility of personal fulfilment or self-actualization' (Conor, Gill, and Taylor, 2015, p.5).

However, for several decades now, research has also looked beyond the individual to incorporate a broader understanding of the concept of creativity in order to account for the impact of the cultures in which the creative individual operates (Abuhamdeh and Csikszentmihalyi, 2004; Rudowicz, 2003). Taking art as a highly creative medium, Korsmeyer (2004) argues that

> images, representations, and crafted expression of ideas are important not only for their beauty, virtuosity, or intrinsic value, but also because they are indicators of social position and power ... art and aesthetic taste are powerful framers of self-image, social identity, and public values.
>
> (p.1)

In other words, the results of the creative process may often be a reflection of societal values and hierarchies, and therefore the contexts in which creativity emerges and becomes manifest warrant careful attention. On this issue, and as a result of vibrant feminist movements in many countries, in more recent decades a concerted grappling with women's historic and continued exclusion from the cultural sphere has foregrounded the issue of sexism and gendered notions of creativity in explaining male dominance of cultural and creative production. Such a focus often has to contend with presumptions that the field of creative practice is devoid of hierarchies along sex, race, and class lines, something referred to as one of the 'myths of equality and diversity in the CCI' (Conor, Gill and Taylor, 2015, p.5). So, what does explain the relative lack of women in creative spheres when compared with their male peers? This question has exercised scholars such as Kogan (1974), who notes that '(w)here creativity refers to task performance on dimensions variously labelled "divergent thinking", "ideational fluency", "associative productivity", "originality", "uniqueness", "spontaneous flexibility", or other related constructs, consistent sex differences have not been found' (p.2). And similarly, more than 30 years later, Keller, Lavish, and Brown (2007) note that there is relatively little research tracking issues of gender and gender roles as linked to creativity. However, having said that, the body of work that does touch on the aspect of sex, gender, and creativity offers some thought-provoking insights, debates, and contradictions.

Gender and creativity: from myths to empirical studies

The side-lining and silencing of women in culture is a long-standing one. Kaplan (2020) recounts a public lecture delivered by British historian and TV personality Professor Mary Beard, where Beard laments such a trend in ancient Greek texts such as Homer's *Odyssey*, which features a passage by Telemachus admonishing his mother to stay out of the affairs of the household since woman's rightful state is one of silence. He proclaims, 'speech will be the business of men' (cited in Kaplan, 2020, p.207). While Beard's criticism of such a pronouncement is that it serves to shut women out of the corridors of power, such stories and narratives – handed down through our cultures over the span of centuries – also work to cement the myth that greatness, be that political, intellectual, or cultural, occurs in the realm of men and not women. In other words, 'the stories our culture tells us of great men ... form faces of the same story of the Hero who confirms masculine narcissism and omnipotence' (Pollock, 1999, p.xxx–xxxi). By the 15th and 16th centuries, the societies of the European Renaissance period conceived of the artist as a 'male creator – one who works alone or directs a crew of underlings, and who, at his very best, possesses the distinctly male trait of "genius"' (Korsmeyer, 2004, p.6). Furthermore, by the following century there was a clear demarcation established whereby the creative practices more typically taken up by women, such as embroidery, were no longer considered to be 'art'.

Such forms of creativity associated with women were deemed to be domestic rather than 'high' art and so came to be termed 'crafts'. This produced a gendered hierarchy of creativity with men associated with 'art', which was to be considered serious, important, genius, and visionary, with women's creative outputs relegated to the realm of 'craft' (Korsmeyer, 2004). Allusions to this hierarchy are plentiful, with Korsmeyer (2004) noting that one does not have to try too hard to find examples of implicit and explicit gendered assumptions about the creative capabilities of men and women. She calls to mind the early 19th-century German philosopher Arthur Schopenhauer's assertion that the skills and temperament needed for creative work are simply outside the scope of what is possible for women but argues that a more insidious and subtle set of ideas about the very nature of innate femininity and masculinity constitute the underlying belief system of such declarations.

This worldview of women's innate feminine inferiority much more firmly took root in the aftermath of the Enlightenment. Opposing viewpoints about sexual difference and whether women were naturally lesser equipped intellectually, spiritually, and creatively than men, such that male dominance was therefore right and natural, ensued during this period. Out of these intellectual debates and ideological tug-of-war, the philosopher Jean-Jacques Rousseau's position advocating an excessive segregation of the sexes won out. He posited that women's limited ability to think or act analytically, rationally, or in a sophisticated way meant that she could never produce great works of art. Instead, her sole *raison d'être* was in the upkeep of the home and the raising of children (Chadwick, 1990). As Chadwick (1990) notes, Rousseau is also to be credited with popularising an equating of women and her associated femininity with the sphere of nature. This was aided by a tendency for binary thinking in explaining the world, with the 'feminine' component of each binary set considered inferior. For instance, emotion, with its associations to femininity and thereby to women, is subordinate to reason, which is considered a masculine and therefore male quality.

The same is the case for 'body' and 'mind', as well as 'nature' and 'culture', which similarly map onto the binary opposites of feminine–female and masculine–male. In explaining this separation of the male realm of mind and culture from women's one of body and nature, Korsmeyer (2004) theorises that we may be able to trace this to a fundamental belief that, while our species considers itself unique among animals in its capacity to think and act rationally and to employ reason, and that such a capacity extends to all people, different groups have historically and throughout different cultures been considered less adept to behave in rational ways. We see this with so-called 'race science' ideologies that sought to 'prove' the superiority of the white 'race' over others in order to justify the system of slavery; and we likewise see such 'proof' put forward – in various cultures, over different points in history – of women's inferior abilities for thinking rationally and intellectually and therefore creatively. In other words, 'in numerous theoretical contexts reason is considered the chief trait that elevates male over female within our species' (Korsmeyer, 2004, p.12) since women, despite a capacity for rationality as a result of her status as human being, is nevertheless, because of her biology, inevitably more aligned with what is more bodily and therefore non-rational. This is to say that those abilities that raise us above other animals are understood to be broadly human, but specifically tied to male capacities; such abilities are framed in opposition to 'feminine' ones. However, where expedient to do so, Korsmeyer (2004) notes, men will and indeed do claim 'feminine' traits, especially in the realm of art, culture, and creative practice, which are all more generally understood and described in terms connected to the sphere of the body and emotion rather than conceived as purely rational or intellectual.

The puzzle of why, if creativity has connotations more typically associated with the feminine, women are not the sex considered more suited to such practice is explained by an essentialist belief that women's apparent closeness to nature and to her reproductive function negates her ability to think, act, and create beyond '*pro*creativity' (p.14). Therefore, 'free from biological destiny' (ibid.), the ability to harness the corporeality, imagination, and emotion necessary in creative endeavour belongs to men. In a similar vein, Pollock (2003) decries 'Western phallocentric monoculture' (p.xxi–xxii) and places the blame for men's hoarding of artistic and creative self-congratulations in the way that femininity, and by extension women themselves, are constructed as 'deficient' (p.xxi), which therefore legitimises women's exclusion and naturalises men's claiming of artistic involvement only for their own sex.

A role that women are not excluded from fulfilling, however, is that of the 'muse', typically understood to be one of 'nine female figures who embody the spirit of some art form and figuratively inspire a (male) human creator' (Korsmeyer, 2004, p.19). However, as Korsmeyer argues, conceiving of creative inspiration as a female 'muse' does not amount to a recognition of women's creative capacities. Rather it represents a strategy which serves to alienate women further from creative and artistic practice. In other words, where feminine creative works or powers were acknowledged and celebrated, they tended to be embodied with mythical female figures in the guise of the 'muse' instead of real-life, living women. Furthermore, as Matson (1993) suggests, since the relationship between the male creator and his 'divine female partner' (p.20) or 'muse' was often framed in a romantic and sometimes sexual sense, it is not surprising that women artists and creatives did not typically report having the same concept of the 'muse' as a source of inspiration. Matson quotes from Robert Graves's *The White Goddess* from 1948:

> woman is not a poet: she is either a Muse or she is nothing. This is not to say that a woman should refrain from writing poems; only, that she should write as a woman, not as if she were an honorary man ... A woman who concerns herself with poetry should, I believe, either be a silent Muse and inspire the poets by her womanly presence, as Queen Elizabeth and the Countess of Derby did, or she should be the Muse in a complete sense ... She should be the visible moon: impartial, loving, severe, wise. (446–7)
>
> (cited in Matson, 1993, p.20)

Matson takes exception to Graves's view of women, but not his assertion that the sexes of the poet/muse cannot be reversed because – for Matson – there are fundamental biological distinctions between men and women that direct their relationship to their sources of inspiration (whether divine or otherwise). Theories of psychoanalysis can help us understand this, in the sense that a woman is understood as operating in 'relational' ways where she conceives of herself in connection with others, whereas the psychological developmental stages that a male goes through result in seeing himself as apart, alone, and 'independent'. As such, the male artist or poet looks for inspiration outside himself; he looks to be 'impregnated' (p.21) with creative powers and ideas if and when the muse comes. For a woman, however, since she is already strongly in tune with herself as connected to others and crucially as inseparable from the figure of the mother, she understands herself as capable of gestating new and original creative works.

While such an essentialist position runs counter to much feminist scholarship which expressly seeks to decouple women from biological deterministic beliefs about women's supposed innate relationality and closeness to the body, Matson (1993) raises an interesting point about the need for women to construct an alternative 'model of ... creativity ... that is female-centered' (p.22). In one respect, such an alternative model of women's creativity may need to address the issue of legacy, given that for each generation of creative women, there is a distinct feeling of having to position oneself as a pioneer and as breaking new ground. This work of attempting to connect women across the span of time and generations falls to feminists, with Schapiro characterising these efforts in terms that 'each generation opens the wounds, which close in the night behind them' (cited in Humphries, 2010, p.179). In other words, in seeking to counter the effects of men preventing, in large part, women's 'access to the symbolic order' (Chadwick, 1990, p.34) and similarly of inclusion in a creative and artistic canon, women have strived to construct a narrative of female creativity where she can locate her own creative drive, passion, talent, and practice.

This challenge speaks to the relative invisibility of female creativity in our cultures and is an issue that is still relevant in contemporary society. The scholar and critic Camille Paglia opined in 1990 that 'if civilization had been left in female hands, we would still be living in grass huts' (cited in Cameron, 2018, p.103). As Cameron notes, this viewpoint is simply a rehashing of the centuries old belief that because of women's role as the sex who is capable of reproduction, she cannot – and has not – been involved in creating great works of art or literature nor advanced the fields of engineering, medicine, or architecture, for instance. Indeed, Korsmeyer (2004) regrets that assumptions of the artist-creator as male still apply in the contemporary period, something she suggests has persevered, despite the gains made by women in society, because of the power of subconscious, long-standing beliefs about the supposed natural and differential capacities of men and women.

Outside the sphere of philosophical or psychoanalytic theorising, some scholarship has also centred the question of whether sex has a role to play in creative competence, and how gender might operate in ways that might shape or impact on women's creativity. However, this is still a relatively underexplored topic in research, with Selby, Shaw, and Houtz (2005) noting that most creativity research traditionally only focused on men. Similarly, in their review of a range of research studies on gender differences in creativity, Baer and Kaufman (2008) point to the lack of attention given to this subject. Indeed, they say, given that 'the differences in real-world creative accomplishment are large and significant ... it is here that explanations are most needed' (p.76). In other words, concerted scholarship needs to centre questions of sex, gender, and creativity in order to gather evidence and data so that reasons as to women's under-performance and under-achievement in creative fields, relative to men, may be put forward. They argue that, armed with such insights and information, it would be possible to address the persistent sex imbalance and the 'waste of human creative talent' (p.76) by tackling the spheres of, for instance, education as well as industry and field-specific recognition and rewards. On this issue of wasted talents, Helson and Pals (2000) also note that research into women and creativity remains a 'neglected subject' (p.24) and position their own study as one which seeks to highlight the challenge and benefits of ensuring that 'potential' in creative women culminates in creative achievement, while Reis (2002) similarly centres the issue of creative 'productivity' but points out that 'little is known about diverse, creative women, the choices they make, and the decisions they face' (p.305).

Nevertheless, in reviewing the literature that does exist, Baer and Kaufman (2008) conclude that across a range of studies exploring various aspects of creativity, 'there is a consistent lack of gender differences both in creativity scores and in the creative accomplishments of boys and girls (which if anything tend to favor girls)' (p.75). This further begs the question of why the chasm in creative accomplishment skews in favour of men later in life. Different scholars have sought to explain such differences through either biology (nature), environment (nurture), or both. In relation to biological explanations, Baer and Kaufman (2008) reference Vernon's (1989) assertion that social factors alone could not account for the large discrepancy in creative achievement of men relative to women and that therefore 'genetic factors' must play a role. What others have pulled Vernon up on, however, is that they consider that he does not give due regard to the extent of sex-based discrimination and differential gender socialisation and expectations. For instance, Baer and Kaufman note that Simonton (1994) argued that at least three other factors have led men and women to compete for acclaim on an uneven playing field: different socialisation practices for girls and boys, different costs of marriage and family for men and women, and the effects of a 'gender ambience of a particular civilization at a given time ... not very sympathetic to female attainments' (cited in Baer and Kaufman, 2008, p.92).

Reis (2002) also references scholarship that sets out to explain the dearth of female creatives and notes that some scholars (see Gates, 1994; cited in Reis, 2002, p.305–306) put forward a 'variability hypothesis' or 'the mediocrity of women hypothesis' (ibid.) to suggest that women may naturally simply be more middling or average than men. Steven Pinker similarly puts forward evidence of studies to show this greater 'variance' in creative and intellectual achievement among men relative to women, something referred to as the trend for 'more prodigies, more idiots' (Baer and Kaufman, 2008, p.92) among men. As a counter-perspective, other scholars have centred the issue of gendered socialisation and sex-role stereotyping in the lives of creative girls and women (Helson, 1999; Reis, 2002) to account for sex-based differences in creative achievements. Helson's (1999) three decades' longitudinal study, which began tracking over 100 college women in 1967, argues that the traditionalist gendered norms and social conditions in which her cohort of young women were born and raised in the 1950s and 1960s in the US very strongly sold them the message that 'women gave birth to babies' (p.90), not creative ideas and pieces of work. Meanwhile, Reis (2002) points out that sex-role stereotyping, sexism, and the pressures of managing creative work with the demands of a family life have impacted greatly on the ability of creative women to fulfil their potential. In other words, the findings of her study indicate that the trajectory of the lives of the women can, and indeed often does, work against being involved in creative practice, whether professionally or personally. Such issues are also at the heart of this book's exploration of women and their creative lives.

The following chapters discuss the childhoods and upbringings of these women. The next chapter, Chapter 2, provides a discussion of the finding that the aspect of freedom and of having, for the most part, parents who are not overly interested or invested in the creative pursuits of their daughters is critical in fostering a conducive environment to explore their burgeoning creativity as girls and teenagers. Chapter 3 highlights the importance of learning and growing in the higher education environment. Through the faith shown in their creative abilities by important mentors in their young adulthood and early career years, the women are able to confidently grasp opportunities as they presented themselves. The next chapter, Chapter 4, deals with themes uncovered in connection to their creative work and practice. Particularly, the extent to which issues connected to sex and gender are unpacked, as is the evidence among this study's cohort of a very strong work ethic, a robust resilience, and a determination to persist. The chapter closes in considering how motherhood, for those women who have children but also those who do not, plays a role in approaches to creative work. Chapter 5 outlines the importance of creativity in the lives of these women and the feelings of joy, satisfaction, and fulfilment that they garner from their work. It was found that the women had all constructed a very strong creative identity which is crucial in sustaining them in their creative work. The book closes with Chapter 6, reflecting on some of the main findings of the study and a summary and overview of the central ideas, theories, and concepts that underpin the work, as well as offering some brief and tentative suggestions for ensuring the future nurturing of girls' and women's creativity.

Note

1 The women who took part in this study were selected because they are involved in a broad range of creative work and practices, from those on the fine art side of the creative and cultural industries to those in more commercial creative fields. Additionally, they represent several generations of Irish women, ranging in age from their late 80s (Lelia Doolan) and their early 50s to early 60s (Amanda Coogan, Liz O'Kane, Una Healy, Lisa Mulcahy, Marina Carr, Carole Pollard, and Annie West) to their 30s and 40s (Jess Kavanagh and Oonagh Kearney). Below are brief profiles of these women. More information can be found on their respective and other websites:

Amanda Coogan, performance art:
'Amanda is an internationally recognised and critically acclaimed artist working across the medias of live art, performance, photography and video. She is one of the most dynamic and exciting contemporary visual artists practicing in the arena of performance ... Coogan holds a degree in Sculpture from Dublin's National College of Art and Design. She was a Masters student of Marina Abramovic at the Hochschule fur Bildende Kunst in Braunschweig, Germany and was awarded her PhD "Deconstructing and Reconstructing live Durational Performance in the Gallery" from the University of Ulster in 2013. She is an occasional lecturer at the National College of Art and Design, Dublin; Limerick School of Art and Design; The Institute of Art, Design and Technology, Dublin; Dublin Institute of Technology and Crawford College of Art, Cork'.
Source: http://www.amandacoogan.com/about.html

Annie West, illustration:
'Born in 1961, Annie graduated from Dun Laoghaire College of Art & Design (IADT) in 1979 with a Diploma in Design for Communications. She began working in the Design Department at RTÉ and Tyne Tees Television and various independent TV productions for Channel Four. This was followed by a decade working in the Art Department on feature films in Ireland, Britain and America. Around 1991 Annie left the Film & TV industry to concentrate on illustrating and cartooning full time. She specialises in highly detailed pen and ink drawings with the emphasis on detail ... Annie has won a number of Awards: The Alfred Beit Award in 1993 & 1994, The NCEA Patent Practitioners' Award 1994, and the Illustrators' Guild Best Book Illustration Award 2003 & 2004'.
Source: https://www.anniewest.com/about

Carole Pollard, architecture:
A graduate of Dublin School of Architecture, DIT with a MA (Hons) in History of Design from the National College of Art and Design, Dublin, Carole describes her architectural practice as including 'research, writing and lecturing on architectural history with a particular focus on the twentieth century. I

have been an active member of the RIAI since 1992 when I helped establish the RIAI Small Practice Forum. In 1998 I set up a network and support group for architects working part-time. I was Convenor of the RIAI Professional Practice Examination from 2004 until its cessation in 2014 and currently teach and examine on the Professional Diploma in Architectural Practice programme at DIT. I am a Professional Studies (RIBA Part 3) examiner at Queens University Belfast. I am Design Studio tutor in 2nd Year Architecture at DIT and an occasional visiting lecturer/reviewer at the other Irish schools of architecture. As RIAI President 2016/17 I was committed to supporting sustainable careers in architecture, to raising the profile of architecture in Ireland, and to promoting the relevance of architects in the creation of a quality built environment and I continue to support and promote those aims through my position on RIAI Council and other platforms'.
Source: https://www.linkedin.com/in/carole-pollard-friai-0bb2b737/?original Subdomain=ie

Jess Kavanagh, music:
'Jess Kav has been a key figure in creative communities in Ireland and abroad and a prominent fixture in the Irish music scene. Raised by an Irish-Nigerian mother and Soul enthusiast, she was fed a musical diet of Motown, Jazz and Irish Indie. After studying at London's Institute Of Contemporary Music Performance and Dún Laoghaire Institute of Art, Design and Technology, Jess has focused on songwriting, touring, recording, writing and social change. Jess has toured worldwide as a backing vocalist with The Waterboys, while also writing and releasing music with original band BARQ until 2020. She has previously worked with top Irish and international artists including Hozier, Villagers, Kodaline, The Commitments, Jape and Le Galaxie and has collaborated with top brands including Google, Amazon, Diageo, Twitter, Jameson, Audi and Smithwicks'.
Source: https://www.jesskavmusic.com/

Lelia Doolan, theatre, TV, and film:
'Doolan was born in Cork in 1934. She studied French and German at University College Dublin, where she won a scholarship to study at the Brecht Theatre in Germany. She presented and acted in shows on the newly established RTÉ in 1961 and starred in a short entertainment called "The Ballad Singer" produced by Tom McGrath, a program preserved in the station's archives.[1] She soon moved into a role as producer/director after training in the United States. She was responsible for the establishment of *The Riordans* rural soap opera … Shortly after being made head of light entertainment, Doolan resigned in protest at the political and commercial policies of RTÉ. She became artistic director of the Abbey Theatre for two years before studying for her PhD in Anthropology at Queen's University. While she was there, she also worked in community video and adult education in Belfast … She taught at the College of Commerce, Rathmines (now part of the DIT) between 1979 and 1988, where she established and was head of the first Irish course in Media Communications … In 1987 she produced *Reefer and the Model*, with director Joe Comerford. In April 1993 she was appointed chairperson of the Irish Film Board, a role she filled for three years before retiring.[4] She was also a founder and director of the Galway Film Fleadh'.
Source: https://en.wikipedia.org/wiki/Lelia_Doolan

Lisa Mulcahy, TV and film:
'Lisa Mulcahy is an award-winning writer and director. Having directed numerous TV dramas and documentaries including *On Home Ground, Raging Bulls, The Clinic*, and *Dan, Dad & Me*, her first feature film, *Situations Vacant*, was released in 2009 to acclaim ... In 2015, Mulcahy won an IFTA Gala Television Award for her direction of the hit TV3 drama *Red Rock*, which also won Best Soap and The People's Choice Award on the same night. Also in 2015, Mulcahy wrote and directed the epic fantasy film *The Legend of Longwood* which follows a 12-year-old New York girl (Lucy Morton) who moves to a quaint village in Ireland, but soon discovers an ancient mystery about the Black Knight that haunts the town. Mulcahy directed BBC mini-series Ridley Road, for which she received an IFTA nomination for Best Director – Drama in 2022'.
Source: https://ifta.ie/academy_members/mp/lisa_mulcahy.html

Liz O'Kane, sculpture:
'Elizabeth O'Kane is a sculptor and painter, originally from Northern Ireland, now working in Dublin. Her work follows the realist tradition. Her sculptures are figurative and focus on anatomy, portraiture, and movement. She works in bronze and stone. Her watercolours are strongly architectural, delicately painted onto carefully drafted drawings. Detailed cityscapes set in strong sunlight and bold shadows offer a sculptural, photorealist style. Originally a French translator, travel is a recurrent theme. Over a twenty year career Elizabeth has exhibited at the Royal Ulster Academy and the Royal Hibernian Academy of Art (where she won the RHA Conor/Moran Sculpture Award) and has been an invited artist at both. She is a member of The Art Students League of New York, the Water Colour Society of Ireland and the Ulster Watercolour Society. Elizabeth's work can be found in various public and private collections, including The Irish Embassy in Washington DC, The Department of Foreign Affairs and Trade, The National Library of Ireland, The National Concert Hall, University of Limerick, University College Dublin and Shannon Airport'.
Source: https://elizabethokane.com/

Marina Carr, theatre playwright:
'Marina Carr is an Irish playwright. She has written almost thirty plays, including By the Bog of Cats (1998) which was revived at the Abbey Theatre in 2014. Carr was born in Dublin, Ireland but she spent the majority of her childhood in Pallas Lake, County Offaly, adjacent to the town of Tullamore. Carr's father, Hugh Carr, was a playwright and studied music under Frederick May, while her mother, Maura Eibhlín Breathnach, was the principal of the local school and wrote poetry in Irish. It was said that "there were a lot of literary rivalries". As a child, Carr and her siblings built a theater in their shed. Carr attended University College Dublin, studying English and philosophy. She graduated in 1987, and subsequently received an honorary degree of Doctorate of Literature from her alma mater. She has held posts as writer-in-residence at the Abbey Theatre, and has taught at Trinity College Dublin, Princeton University, and Villanova University. She lectured in the English department at Dublin City University in 2016. Marina Carr is considered one of Ireland's most prominent playwrights and is a member of Aosdána. Her works have been translated into many languages, and have received much critical acclaim'.
Source: https://en.wikipedia.org/wiki/Marina_Carr

Oonagh Kearney, theatre and film:
'Oonagh Kearney has written and directed nine short films and one full-length arts documentary with the support of the Irish Arts Council, Irish Film Board, RTE, TG4, BRITDOC and The Welcome Trust. Her work has screened globally at over one hundred film festivals around the world, at the ICA in London, BFI, IFI and as part of the 2014 Art on the London Underground Series ... Nominated for Best Emerging International Filmmaker, Oonagh was awarded special mention at The London Open City Docs Festival in 2013. Oonagh first cut her teeth in film as casting director to Ken Loach on his Palm d'Or winning film "The Wind That Shakes the Barley" in 2005. She trained at the National Film and Television School in London before casting five more feature films. Since 2010, she has focused on writing and directing. For two years, she taught film part-time at the University of Suffolk. She holds a 1st class honours BA in English and Philosophy from University College Cork and 1st Class honours MPhil. in Irish Theatre from Trinity College Dublin. Oonagh's interest in the politics of representation can be traced to her Irish Film Board short "The Christening" that tells the story of an Irish teenager traveling to London for an abortion. Oonagh takes a playful approach to the impact of family, and the tension between our private and public selves. In her dance and narrative films, women often experience emotional or ethical conflicts connected to rites of passage'.
Source: https://filmfreeway.com/OonaghKearney

Una Healy, graphic design:
An award-winning brand and graphic designer, Una notes that 'I have always loved making and designing. From a very early age I was drawing and designing. It was something that has always been part of my life. At 14, I realised I could make money from drawing caricatures. After school I studied Visual Communications in IADT. On leaving college, there were no jobs for design graduates in Ireland. I moved to London and began working with agencies there. By year 3, I was being head hunted by graphic design studios, yet I wanted to come home to Ireland. We were still in recession. The only way to come home was to set up a business. Not a great time for any startup! On returning home, I worked on various design projects, as people approached me to help with their businesses. I illustrated children's books, designed brands for businesses etc. Work grew organically, until it became a full-time operation''.
Source: https://www.localenterprise.ie/DublinCity/Case-Studies/Una-Healy -Design.html
See also: https://www.unahealydesign.com/

References

Abuhamdeh, S. and Csikszentmihalyi, M. (2004) 'The artistic personality: A systems perspective', in Sternberg, R.J., Grigorenko, E.L. and Singer, J.L. (eds.) *Creativity: From potential to realization*. Washington, DC: American Psychological Association, pp. 31–42.

Baer, J. and Kaufman, J.C. (2008) 'Gender differences in creativity', *Journal of Creative Behavior*, 42(2), pp. 75–105. https://doi.org/10.1002/j.2162-6057.2008 .tb01289.x.

Cameron, D. (2018) *Feminism*. London: Profile Books.

Chadwick, W. (1990) *Women, art, and society*. London: Thames and Hudson.

Conor, B., Gill, R. and Taylor, S. (2015) 'Introduction: Gender and creative labour', in Conor, B., Gill, R. and Taylor, S. (eds.) *Gender and creative labour*. Chichester: Wiley-Blackwell, pp. 1–23.

Crowley, F. (2017) 'Irish policymakers must focus more on the creative sector', *RTÉ Brainstorm*, 22 November. Available at: https://www.rte.ie/brainstorm/2017 /1121/921676-irish-policymakers-must-focus-more-on-the-creative-sector/ (Accessed: 4 April 2022).

DCMS (Department for Culture, Media and Sport) (2001) 'Creative Industries Mapping Document, London', Available from http://www.culture.gov.uk/ Reference_library/Publications/archive_2001/ci_mapping_doc_2001.htm. Last Accessed 8 May 2008.

Gates, E. (1994) 'Why have there been no great women composers? Psychological theories, past and present', *Journal of Aesthetic Education*, 28(2), pp. 27–34.

Gross, J.D. (2020) *The birth of the creative industries revisited: An oral history of the 1998 DCMS mapping document*. London: King's College London. Available at: https://www.kcl.ac.uk/cultural/resources/reports/the-birth-of-the-creative -industries-revisited.pdf (Accessed: 4 April 2022).

Grow, J.M. and Deng, T. (2015) 'Tokens in a man's world: Women in creative advertising departments', *Media Report to Women*, 43(1), pp. 6–23.

Helson, R. (1965) 'Childhood interest clusters related to creativity in women', *Journal of Consulting Psychology*, 29(4), pp. 352–361. https://doi.org/10.1037 /h0022401.

Helson, R. (1966) 'Personality of women with imaginative and artistic interests: The role of masculinity, originality, and other characteristics in their creativity', *Journal of Personality*, 34(1), pp. 1–25. https://doi.org/10.1111/j.1467-6494 .1966.tb01695.x.

Helson, R. (1999) 'A longitudinal study of creative personality in women', *Creativity Research Journal*, 12(2), pp. 89–101. https://doi.org/10.1207/s15326934crj1202_2.

Helson, R. and Pals, J.L. (2000) 'Creative potential, creative achievement, and personal growth', *Journal of Personality*, 68(1), pp. 1–27. https://doi.org/10 .1111/1467-6494.00089.

Henry, C. (2009) 'Women and the creative industries: Exploring the popular appeal', *Creative Industries Journal*, 2(2), pp. 143–160. https://doi.org/10.1386/cij.2.2 .143/1.

Hesmondhalgh, D. and Baker, S. (2011) 'Introduction: Can creative labour be good work?' in Hesmondhalgh, D. and Baker, S. (eds.) *Creative labour: Media work in three cultural industries*. Abingdon, Oxon; New York: Routledge, pp. 52–78.

Hesmondhalgh, D. and Baker, S. (2015) 'Sex, gender and work segregation in the cultural industries', in Conor, B., Gill, R. and Taylor, S. (eds.) *Gender and creative labour*. Chichester: Wiley-Blackwell, pp. 23–36.

Humphries, J. (2010) 'Re(writing) the domestic in the everyday', in O'Connor, E. (ed.) *Irish women artists, 1800–2009*. Dublin: Four Courts Press, pp. 179–195.

Kaplan, J. (2020) *The genius of women: From overlooked to changing the world.* Dutton: Penguin Random House.

Kaufman, J.C. and Baer, J. (2004) 'Hawking's Haiku, Madonna's Math: Why it is hard to be creative in every room of the house', in Sternberg, R.J., Grigorenko, E.L. and Singer, J.L. (eds.) *Creativity: From potential to realization.* Washington, DC: American Psychological Association, pp. 3–19.

Keller, C.J., Lavish, L.A. and Brown, C. (2007) 'Creative styles and gender roles in undergraduate students', *Creativity Research Journal,* 19(2–3), pp. 273–280.

Kogan, N. (1974) 'Creativity and sex differences', *Journal of Creative Behavior,* 8 (1), pp. 1–14.

Korsmeyer, C. (2004) *Gender and aesthetics: An introduction.* New York: Routledge.

Liddy, S. (2020) 'Setting the scene: Women in the Irish film industry', in Liddy, S. (ed.) *Women in the Irish film industry: Stories and storytellers.* Cork: Cork University Press, pp. 1–14.

Lubart, T. and Guignard, J.H. (2004) 'The generality-specificity of creativity: A multivariate approach', in Sternberg, R.J., Grigorenko, E.L. and Singer, J.L. (eds.) *Creativity: From potential to realization.* Washington, DC: American Psychological Association, pp. 43–56.

Matson, S. (1993) 'Disquieting Muses: Mnemosyne', *Harvard Review,* 5, pp. 20–22.

McCracken, K., FitzSimons, A., Priest, S., Girstmair, S. and Murphy, B. (2018) *Gender equality in the media sector.* Brussels: European Parliament. Available at: https://www.europarl.europa.eu/RegData/etudes/STUD/2018/596839/IPOL _STU(2018)596839_EN.pdf (Accessed: 4 April 2022).

Milestone, K. (2015) 'Gender and the cultural industries', in Oakley, K. and O'Connor, J. (eds.) *The Routledge companion to the cultural industries.* London and New York: Routledge, pp. 501–511.

Niu, W. and Sternberg, R.J. (2006) 'The philosophical roots of Western and Eastern conceptions of creativity', *Journal of Theoretical and Philosophical Psychology,* 26(1–2), pp. 18–38. https://doi.org/10.1037/h0091265.

Oliveira, E. (2018) *An analysis of the cultural and creative industries in Ireland: Implications for policy-making.* PG diploma thesis. DIT School of Marketing. Available at: https://www.researchgate.net/publication/327655739 (Accessed: 4 April 2022).

Pollock, G. (1999) *Differencing the Canon: feminist desire and the writing of art's histories.* Abington: Routledge.

Pollock, G. (2003) *Vision and difference: Feminism, femininity and the histories of art.* London and New York: Routledge.

Reis, S.M. (2002) 'Toward a theory of creativity in diverse creative women', *Creativity Research Journal,* 14(3–4), pp. 305–316. https://doi.org/10.1207/ S15326934CRJ1434_2.

Rudowicz, E. (2003) 'Creativity and Culture: A two way interaction', *Scandinavian Journal of Educational Research,* 47(3), pp. 273–290. https://doi.org/10.1080 /00313830308602.

Schweizer, T.S. (2006) 'The psychology of novelty-seeking, creativity and innovation: Neurocognitive aspects within a work-psychological perspective',

Creativity and Innovation Management, 15(2), pp. 164–172. https://doi.org/10.1111/j.1467-8691.2006.00383.x.

Selby, E.C., Shaw, E.J. and Houtz, J.C. (2005) 'The creative personality', *Gifted Child Quarterly*, 49(4), pp. 300–314. https://doi.org/10.1177/001698620504900404.

Taylor, M. and O'Brien, D. (2017) 'Culture is a meritocracy: Why creative workers' attitudes may reinforce social inequality', *Sociological Research Online*, pp. 1–21. https://doi.org/10.1177/1360780417726732.

Vernon, P.E. (1989) 'The nature-nurture problem in creativity', in Glover, J.A., Ronning, R.R. and Reynolds, C.R. (eds.) *Handbook of creativity: Perspectives on individual differences*. New York: Plenum Press, pp. 93–110.

Windels, K. and Lee, W.N. (2012) 'The construction of gender and creativity in advertising creative departments', *Gender in Management: An International Journal*, 27(8), pp. 502–519.

Windels, K. and Mallia, K.L. (2015) 'How being female impacts learning and career growth in advertising creative departments', *Employee Relations: The International Journal*, 37(1), pp. 122–140. https://doi.org/10.1108/ER-02-2014-0011.

Woolf, V. (1929) *A room of one's own*. England: Hogarth Press.

2   Childhood and adolescence
Experiences that foster creativity in girls

The households that the ten women interviewed for this study grew up in share a common experience of having 'un-pushy' parents. As children, their hobbies in art, painting, singing and putting on plays were left as passions and as areas of enjoyment and of fun and play, rather than as skills to improve on. While Jess's upbringing was a more challenging one than the other women in that she had a very strong bond but a somewhat fraught relationship with her mother regarding her singing and involvement with music, and likewise Lisa's childhood is notable for the-then atypical situation of growing up in a single-mother household, her father having left the family home to begin a relationship with another woman, there is a unifying experience across the study cohort of having come from stable and loving households. In addition, these women report, for the most part, having had a significant degree of freedom. This manifests both in physical and psychological ways. In particular, many of the women spoke of running around the countryside or their housing estates from morning to evening over long summer months. This freedom to roam and explore in nature or around their areas speaks to a formative and early sense of feeling empowered to figure out the world and where their interests lay without much, if any, pressure or interference. Where there was influence, it often came in the form of strong encouragement from teachers in school or important figures in their childhood who instilled in them a confidence in their creative and artistic abilities.

Although these women may not have been expressly pushed or directed towards creative lives, and indeed typically the households they grew up in were not completely steeped in culture – in other words, not environments where art and culture were overtly and vigorously consumed or talked about or debated – there was a general open-mindedness among parents about the importance or legitimacy of art and culture. This chapter expands on these common, and sometimes diverging, threads throughout the childhoods and adolescence of these women.

DOI: 10.4324/9781003082750-2

Freedom to explore (psychological and physical)

Featuring strongly as a defining experience in the lives of these women was a licence to spread their wings and to ramble about their neighbourhoods unsupervised as girls and teenagers. Alongside a general sense of having been unrestrained, six of the ten women spoke about how crucial sports were in their formative years, while others reminisced about the sense of being outdoors 'from sunrise to sunset' (Marina Carr) during long summer days. The aspects of moving about freely in their environs and without restrictions and the physical use of the body through sports like running and hockey as well as dance and other kinds of activities seem to have instilled in them a self-confidence and a sense of their own abilities. Lelia recalls that 'you could play in the street, you could play out of doors, you could get up on the horse ... you know, nobody said you couldn't do what you wanted to do really'. Time spent outdoors was fundamental to establishing Lelia's confidence and independence; that she was on the hockey team and also playing cricket with her brothers, as well as cycling herself to school in Dublin, engendered a sense of belonging to the world and of being part of the goings-on around her. In other words, she understood herself to be an active contributor.

Also a hockey player in school, Una Healy engaged in other physical sports and activities such as tap and Irish dancing. She learnt the accordion as a child and as an adult she taught herself piano – all activities and hobbies that she identifies as 'quieter hobbies'. A very shy child, but not solitary, she had lots of good, close friends with whom she hung out and, similar to other interviewees, she talks about the freedom of her childhood to spend the days however she wanted:

> I mean back in those days, sure we'd go out in the mornings and come back for our meals at bedtime, like the freedom was great so we'd huge freedom. So, there would've been less organised things but if we showed any interest in one particular thing they'd certainly back you all the way.

In Liz O'Kane's childhood and adolescence, both art and sport featured heavily, with running, cycling, and tennis and spending time outside being sources of huge enjoyment for her. Although she was not drawn to team sports, her love of drawing and running were activities she carried out with others. In other words, as with Una, Liz engaged with physical and crea-tive activities in shared ways by going to friends' houses to draw together or going running with her father. For Oonagh Kearney, her childhood is painted as one that was very full and active with 'a lot of lifts after school to go to your dancing or go to your thing, like I remember the endless activity of that'. Physicality went hand-in-hand with the more creative pursuits in childhood and adolescence, whereby Oonagh played sport and enjoyed being 'boisterous' with her sisters but also playing with dolls and putting on little plays.

The contribution that physical movement and activity might have made to these women's burgeoning creativity is worth considering. While it remains under-researched, Latorre Román, Pinillos, Pantoja Vallejo, and Berrios Aguayo (2017) suggest that explanations for creativity should be extended beyond an exclusive examination of one's 'internal' or psychological make-up and instead should also include an examination of one's competence with respect to physical activity and fitness. They set out to examine if their study cohort of primary school–age children between 8 and 12 years old (both sexes) with higher fitness levels might show greater capacity for creative thinking, which was determined through a series of exercises designed to measure how well they used their imagination for specific tasks. The authors found that those children who exhibited higher levels of aerobic fitness than their less physically fit peers were also more creative. Furthermore, there were no discernible differences in creativity among the boys and girls. As such, in this study, 'aerobic capacity was a predictor of creativity' (p.1197) rather than sex. This speaks to the importance for girls to get involved in sports and related activities as children and to maintain that involvement into their adolescent and adult years – not just for health reasons but, as indicated by this study, for the cognitive and developmental benefits that results from physical fitness, and for the potential to aid one's imagination and creative functioning.

However, once girls hit puberty and enter adolescence there is an assumption that their involvement with organised sports tends to diminish and they drop away from such pursuits. But worry over this phenomenon might be overstated, especially if very narrow interpretations of 'sport' and 'physical activity' underpin such concerns. Clark, Spence, and Holt (2011) argue that an understanding of such concepts needs to be widened to account for the myriad ways that girls often interact with their bodies and with physical movements and activities. The authors interviewed a small cohort ($n = 8$) of Canadian female students aged from 10 to 13 to consider the role of physical activities in contributing to their confidence and independence as well as providing opportunities to be creative. They found that the girls tended to enjoy the kinds of physical activities that were not overly structured or competitive but rather which gave them opportunities to 'explore their physicality' (p.193) and that appealed to their 'appreciation of movement for movement's sake' (p.203). This aspect of freedom to explore is evident in the ways in which the girls talked about how using their bodies made them feel: 'in girls' experiential accounts of actually being active, discourses of self-expression and creativity emerged' (p.193). In other words, engaging in the kind of free-play that many of them favoured – whether dancing, running around, roller-skating – they reported feeling 'in control' (p.203) and understood that they were directing the enjoyment of such activities. The sense of using one's body in imaginative ways in order to create fun activities and scenarios for oneself and one's friends was vital in developing a range of 'skills', a 'sense of self', and a feeling of 'accomplishment' (p.202) that all contributed to a confidence in themselves.

This certainly tallies with many of the interviewees in this study who fondly remember the joy of running about their neighbourhoods or countryside. Such findings by Clark, Spence, and Holt (2011) also echo the experience of Amanda Coogan, who reports playing sports in school and as being good at hockey, but whose defining experience of her life is that of being a 'CODA' (child of deaf adults). Since sign language is a 'manual productive language' which fundamentally relies on the use of the body in order to communicate and make oneself known and understood, and to understand and connect with others, she credits this early and sustained use of her body in representing a very critical aspect of confidence and identity-building within her and which would later explain her being so drawn to performance art, with the body and physical movement such core elements of that practice.

As suggested by Amanda and others, their relationship to their bodies provided them with creative outlets. Clark, Spence, and Holt (2011) testify to this in stating that self-directed physical play experiences 'provide girls with creative outlets and a means through which they can explore their physical abilities and define competence and ability for themselves' (p.206). And they note that 'experiencing the body through physical activity may be empowering for women and allow them to negotiate traditional gendered identities' (p.205), which is to say that drawing confidence from a relationship with one's body where there's an awareness of what it is capable of and there's a joy garnered from its strength can enable women to reject gendered social norms connected to women and girls' supposed physical vulnerability and frailty. These themes of rejecting vulnerability and instead of embracing the challenges and enjoyment associated with physical activity represent the approach of this study's highly creative cohort.

At 88 years of age and still swimming daily in the Atlantic Ocean off the West of Ireland, Lelia has maintained that link to physical activity throughout her life. Growing up with five siblings, she was sandwiched between a younger and older brother, with whom she hung around with a lot and with whom she played the same games. The countryside was an environment she loved, and she paints a picture of a happy, free, and vibrant childhood with freedom to roam around the countryside when the family visited relatives in

Co. Clare in the summers. Lelia and her siblings would spend three months each summer in rural Clare with her aunt and uncle. During those months, they would help out on the farm but also had opportunities to head 'off on the bikes' to go swimming or cycling out to Lisdoonvarna. The impression left of this time is one of relatively few limits put on them as children, not least physically. Lelia's long and productive career, during which she has worked incredibly hard but always with joy and curiosity, is marked by a boundless generosity and energy for life, fun, and people. The importance of humour, imagination, and a drive to immerse herself in a range of creative activities has, arguably, been sustained by her physical fitness. Marina Carr also has such memories of long days during school holidays with her siblings and other children hanging out by the lake or in the woods. She recalls, 'we had our own world so there was great freedom like that' but it was a freedom that was, in important ways, also lightly supervised, whereby people in the community knew all the kids and looked out for and indeed after them. This ability to explore the physical environment is something that she feels is now missing in the childhoods of children, who are far more curtailed, with parents much more 'fearful'. For girls growing up in our contemporary society, with a more structured approach to filling their after-school hours or with more heavy adult presence and supervision, such freedoms and the associated opportunities for creative play, as enjoyed by this study's cohort, are arguably lost.

The aspect of freedom reported by the women interviewed was also present in a psychological and intellectual sense. A thread, mostly shared, in the upbringing of these women was the flexibility they were afforded to navigate and experiment with different interests without much pressure or interference, particularly from parents. Liz notes that her tastes and her artistic, creative, and cultural interests as a teenager were eclectic and included diverse types of music, cinema, French radio and magazines, dyeing her hair, and altering her clothes, as well as going to gigs and coming up with soundtracks for events in her and her friends' lives. In allowing and enabling their daughters to direct their own spheres of interest, the parents of these women may well have fostered an environment that proved vital in providing psychic space for the girls to creatively explore for themselves. Given the previous discussion on physical freedoms and the central importance of the use of the body in ways that contributed to their confidence in themselves, the parents of this cohort of women have likely – whether intentionally or not – created the conditions most suited to the creative growth of their daughters. As Reis (2002) argues, parents often play a key role in either facilitating or hampering 'the creative process in their children' (p.310). More specifically, as a result of socialising their children into gendered roles and behaviour, some parents may impose on their daughters various rules around appropriate forms of expression and an expected 'feminine' etiquette that would not be imposed on their sons. In practice, this can mean instilling in girls the message that they must be polite and quiet and to consider and prioritise others above oneself, whereas boys get the signal that they are free 'to be independent, autonomous, creative, boisterous, messy' (ibid). Such traits, which are accepted, indeed often encouraged and celebrated, in boys, are those associated with developing and nurturing creativity. Therefore, in seeking to dampen down such traits in their daughters, parents who incorporate a strongly gendered approach risk 'squelching their daughters' enthusiasm and spirit under the guise of manners and behavior codes and sometimes diminishing the passion in their creative spirited daughters' (p.311). Since this has not been the experience of the women in this study, one can conclude that, even though several interviewees reported some gendered expectations on the part of their parents, which will be discussed in later sections, their upbringing has not been characterised by a strictly gendered style of parenting. Instead, as indicated, their childhoods were largely free of heavily gendered notions of appropriate ways of behaving as related to girls. Without such confines, these women, in their youth, could imagine lives for themselves that would foreground creative work and that centred their creative passions – lives, therefore, that were often less traditional than those that their mothers typically lived.

Such was Una's experience, where she keenly felt supported by her parents in whatever she turned her hand to, but reports being largely left to her own devices. Although not from artistic or creative backgrounds themselves, Una's mother and father clearly both had a creative streak in them. Her mother would knit and make clothes; she also baked and loved to sing. Her father enjoyed writing and would write plays for the family to perform at Christmas time. She remembers him reading poetry and teaching his daughters the poems: 'so I suppose when I think of it, yeah, they were creative, but it was considered hobby stuff'. As much as she loved art, she had a sense that pursuing a life as an 'artist' meant 'you're going to be in an attic, painting and starving' but a little enterprise, in secondary school, whereby she made Valentine's cards for classmates to send to each other and she charged them for each card, was a clarifying moment for Una in the sense that it dawned on her that 'oh you can make money doing this!' This aspect of trying things out for yourself and stumbling on what one might be good at is echoed in Marina's experience of her early years of writing as a child, which are characterised by creating plays with inspiration taken from fairy tales and stories from the Bible for the 'gruesome' parts. She notes, 'there was always a witch, there was always some kind of torture, there was always goodies and baddies'. Discussing the fact that she later went on to be a professional playwright, she says it was not a 'lightbulb moment' or something she consciously decided but she suspects that she was moulded by the experiences in her childhood of having a playwright-father and a teacher-mother, resulting in the fact that she eventually became both.

The confidence extracted from undertaking and practising one's preferred form of creativity is evident also in Carole Pollard's discussion of how central art was for her sense of self. She describes a highly creative childhood, where art was 'everything [she] wanted to do all the time'. A move to a Froebel method school and its focus on 'creative writing, drawing, learning through exploring' was a hugely important experience for her and 'sowed the seeds' for her and 'gave [her] self-esteem'. Later, a 'chaotic' environment in her secondary school proved stressful, but the art room became a place of sanctuary, with her art teacher considered an 'anchor' for her. Acting as both anchor and sanctuary in Jess Kavanagh's life was the space of the drama school which she attended from the age of 13. Being involved in this group was clearly a crucial outlet for her, emotionally, socially, and creatively. In looking back at her childhood and early adulthood, she reflects on feeling like her voice didn't fit the usual expected mode for Irish female singers because of her mixed-race background. Indeed, rather than singing in the more typical 'breathy and ethereal' style that might be associated with white, female singers in Ireland, Jess 'had this voice that was kind of you know weighty and soulful and deep', so she felt marked out as different. She also seems to have felt a certain pressure or responsibility to make it as a singer for the sake of her mother, who was a 'wonderful singer' but had 'terrible stage fright'. It is possible that Jess's feelings of empowerment and freedom come in feeling able to forge ahead in a way she maybe felt her mother could not. In acknowledging that it must have been very hard for her mother as 'a black woman living in a tiny village in Wicklow', she also recognises that she was aware of her own experience of living through a difficult childhood:

> I remember thinking to myself at that age being like 'this is a shit childhood' … like what's happening around me is not good … and I knew it could be and I knew that music made me feel good and that I had the confidence in me and I have the drive and I had the cheekiness in me to be a performer.

Jess's independence, creativeness, and precociousness as a girl are traits more typically associated with and encouraged in boys. Given that these characteristics, which endured, form an integral part of her personality and contributed to her fierce determination to make and to live a creative life, it tracks with Reis's (2002) finding that, in adulthood, creative women tend to continue to exhibit traits that are often considered socially undesirable in women. These aspects of 'determination, commitment, assertiveness, risk taking, and the ability to control one's life' (p.311) are evident in Lisa Mulcahy's life and career also. In the context of the difficult decade after her father had left the family when Lisa was ten years old, she reports that her mother found that period very challenging. Along with this, the fact of having five other siblings, and being the youngest, meant that Lisa enjoyed a kind of adolescence free from strict supervision and scrutiny. Her mother trusted that she would not get into trouble if let out with friends at night 'because I didn't really cause hassle'. In this aspect, as with other women interviewed, the reins are left loose enough to allow Lisa to develop a sense of confidence and competence in navigating a home, school, and social environment, but with the security of feeling loved and supported. Parents who employ such an approach, Miller and Gerard (1979) suggest, may be enabling creativity to thrive in their children. They found that '(r) elationships between creative children and their parents tend to be neither overly close emotionally, nor hostile and detached, but marked by respect, independence and freedom' (p.295). This certainly echoes the upbringing of most of this study's participants who, in one way or another, enjoyed bonds with parents characterised as being close but not too close. And for those women who report having somewhat more complicated or fraught relationships with parents, particularly their mothers, their experiences suggest that there was still love and closeness present alongside a significant degree of freedom to follow their own paths.

Love and stability in households, but also 'benign disinterest'

Love and closeness was largely manifest through a stability and security in the home environment of these women as they were growing up. In terms of attention paid to their daughters' creative and artistic talents, in general a kind of benign disinterest is typical of parents, whereby they were not overly involved in pushing their daughters to hone their skills; rather, their hobbies in art, writing, singing, and so on were left as passions and as areas of enjoyment, fun, and play. Lubart and Guignard (2004) attest to the influence that the family environment can play in facilitating creativity in children. They reference studies that have put forward the theory that secure, warm and stable homes, where there is a loose adherence to rules, 'will serve as a base from which risk taking can be attempted' (p.49). As such, children feel able to try out new things and to experiment and explore in ways that allow them to hone creative skills. Oonagh, for instance, describes growing up in a household that was loving and 'supportive' and where, although her parents were not artistic themselves, there was an appreciation for art and culture and she expressly never had the sense that it was not a valuable or valued thing to be interested in and to pursue. The balance between providing for their daughters' creative interests without getting heavily involved might be a crucial one. Domino (1979) found that, along with the pattern of creative children sharing in common the experience of growing up in households were some freedoms are afforded to them to test their independence, there is also the finding that parents get less involved in the creative activities of their children than the parents of less creative children. In other words, Domino identified a trend of 'parents of creative children exhibit(ing) less concern – less concern about providing their children with the appropriate materials for creative endeavors ... less concern with affectional rewards for appropriate behaviour ... (and) less concern with achievement in intellectual cultural activities' (Domino, 1979, p.826). This tracks with the finding of this study that what could be termed a 'benign disinterest' characterises the approach of the parents towards their daughters' creative interests and passions.

Liz's earliest memories consist of her 'always drawing'; this is in a context where art and artistic skill were not present in her family and Liz's talent for drawing was not something necessarily recognised or celebrated by her parents. Similarly, Una remembers drawing and making dolls' houses and furniture from a very young age. She suggests that the creative streak did not come from her parents as such, who may have 'liked seeing art but it wasn't a real thing, you know, it was a hobby'. For Lelia, both parents were champions of intellectual exploration, but they imagined that, with Lelia's interest in languages, she would have pursued a career in international affairs or a similarly 'useful' job but, says Lelia, 'I seemed to be drawn in the other direction'. Annie West reports that she was not really encouraged at home, where the environment was more geared towards engineering and academic pursuits. In general, Annie suggests she was, in respect of her studies and eventual decision to pursue a creative career path, ignored by parents and family. Her framing of her time at school as one where she was not disruptive but was a bit of a dreamer and was 'always scribbling' indicates that she naturally found her way to art by herself. In choosing art as a subject for the Leaving Certificate Examinations, Annie frames the choice as a continuation of her 'dossing', and not reflective of a serious passion or motivation to pursue some kind of artistic or creative career. The careers counsellor in her school was likewise dismissive but nevertheless advised her to apply to some art schools since it seemed clear that Annie was not academically inclined. Indeed, Annie remembers her being told that she would 'not ... amount to anything so you may as well go to art school'. This speaks to the undervaluing of the arts at the time but also to the potential, unintended positive effect that this disinterest – at home and at school – in Annie's creative achievements arguably had on Annie's determination to see where her creativity might take her.

The experience of Liz, Lelia, and Annie, as well as Oonagh, Marina, Una, and others, in being left to construct their own sense of what their creativity meant in their lives calls to mind the findings across a broad swathe of studies in the field of creative personality research which suggest, in part, that judgement from others can negatively impinge on creative growth. This can be especially detrimental if outside assessment of one's creative outputs is imposed at too early an age. Selby, Shaw, and Houtz (2005) review the literature in this area and note that studies by Amabile and others found that '(p)remature external evaluation stifles one's willingness to express new ideas and may destroy intrinsic motivation and self-confidence' (p.303). In other words, they say, the aspects of 'psychological safety and freedom', something that this study's cohort appear to have enjoyed, are vital in ensuring that individuals feel able to take risks – a crucial component of creativity – without fear that they may disappoint or lose the respect and love of parents and those close to them. Amanda, for instance, was afforded creative freedom but this was coupled with safety in the way her parents stepped in when they felt her best interests were not being served. In particular, she had some early film acting success at the ages of 12 and 13, but since her parents were not comfortable with the idea of her missing too much school, her auditions and commitments to acting were put on hold. Amanda seems to have taken this early success, and the curtailing of those activities, in her stride.

While their parents' mild indifference to their creativity arguably enabled these women to simply get on with exploring their burgeoning creative interests as girls and teenagers, what does seem to have been present in their lives, and may have been a factor in implicitly encouraging their creative sides, was the availability of cultural texts to consume. Some studies on creativity suggest that social class and the exposure of children to art and culture at a young age positively foster creativity. Koppman (2016) developed the concept of 'cultural omnivorousness', which she defines as 'diverse and inclusive' (p.291) eclectic cultural tastes, to suggest that social class may play a factor in the likelihood of children of middle-class parents receiving a cultural education that is characterised by being exposed to a wide range of cultural texts. While this cultural exposure that such parents provide to their children might not result in higher levels of creativity in their children, their acquired cultural knowledge is, Koppman argues, read as equating to creativity and can result in them enjoying an advantage in seeking employment in creative fields. Lubart and Guignard (2004) note that some research has found that the ability to provide a cultural education through 'books, magazines, and cultural activities' can stimulate creativity by exposing children to new ideas and experiences (p.49), while Miller and Gerard (1979) note that, for the most part, creativity researchers find that 'social class is positively related to creativity' (p.302). The opportunity to consume culture in the households in which they grew up is referenced by several interviewees. However, social class may be less factor than simply the availability of cultural products that were readily available and affordable. Lisa remembers a house where music and socialising were very important. Her mother loved rock 'n' roll as well as classical music. The radio 'would always be on' and the household was filled with books; her mother, in particular, was a voracious reader. But at the same time, it was an environment where culture was simply consumed rather than debated or intellectualised, something that tallies with the findings of this study and the literature around creative endeavour not being overly pushed. Indeed, she paints a picture of a lot of life and fun, alongside the hardship of the realities of a single-parent household, where her older brothers were running a hugely successful disco, which sparked in 12-year-old Lisa a sense of excitement and of starting to look out into the world with curiosity and expectation. Cultivating an ability to listen, as the youngest of a large family, she believes marked the beginning of her ability to pay attention to people and their stories, which she'd later bring into her career as a film and television director. As she notes,

> One of the things that I think probably has led me to directing or a tool that I developed as a child was that when you're the youngest in a lively household that was particularly keen on slagging each other … you do not put your head above the parapet because you're the one … that everybody is going to fire the bullets at, right? And so I suppose I developed or maybe I was this naturally but I was a good listener … I always liked watching people maybe because I was forced to because I didn't have a voice, but I always was interested in watching people and listening to people.

This testifies to the dual aspect of cultural influence and opportunity for creative outlets in her upbringing alongside being left, largely, to figure things out for herself. The importance of a variety of cultural influences, or a cultural omnivorousness, as Koppman puts it, seems to have been critical in the creative education of Jess also. Through her access to various local pirate radio stations, doors were opened to her and would result in her spending lots of time in her bedroom singing and dancing to rock, pop, and dance music. The aspect of hanging around Temple Bar in Dublin city – an important city space for adolescents into the grunge and rock music scene in the mid-1990s–2000s – seems to have been really formative for her. She also talks about going to 'all-ages gigs from when I was about 15'. Her mother's working in Whelan's music bar was an important access point for live music gigs. She vividly remembers the experience of shopping for an outfit in Topshop for the after-party of the MTV Video Music Awards in Dublin. It's significant that she's aware of having 'loved the scene, (and) I loved being seen, I loved dressing up and being in these cool places ... I loved the status of it'. For Jess and others, this early exploration of art, culture and experiencing the fact that people could be creative in a variety of ways speaks the influence it may have had on their conception of creativity.

As discussed, factors to do with the home environment as being warm and stable and not overly strict, coupled with their parents providing some cultural education to their daughters while also allowing their children to get on with it without an overbearing involvement, have been crucial experiences for these women. In addition, paying attention to their relationships with their mothers and fathers reveal, in some instances, diverging dynamics. Studies into the influence of distinct temperaments of mothers and fathers on children's creativity, or indeed whether certain characteristics in parents are indicators of their likelihood to have creative children, differ somewhat. Helson (1999), in her longitudinal study into the creative personalities of women, finds some evidence that the parents of women with strong IA (imaginative-artistic) traits tended, like their daughters, to be complex, emotional, and somewhat volatile as well as reporting often experiencing tension in relations with others. While fathers of her study's cohort viewed themselves as more 'argumentative' and 'strict' than 'peaceable ... affectionate and responsive' (p.92), the mothers of Helson's female creative participants considered themselves as 'irritable and touchy and less frequently as adaptable, forgiving, pleasant, and unselfish' (p.92), with the women themselves reporting that their mothers were 'moody' more often than non-IA women who tended to use terms such as 'loyal (and) nurturant' (p.92). This suggests that creative women might be influenced by the experience of having parents who are not overly nurturing, emotional, or self-sacrificing. This echoes other studies, such as referenced in Miller and Gerard (1979) which point to the importance of the 'optimal family pattern for developing creativity as an open but not overly close family with little clinging or conformity, in which the father interacts strongly with children, and the parents easily accept regressions' (p.309). Other studies, such as Foster (1968) and Dewing (1970), who both put forward the theory that children's creativity is best served by growing up in households which operate on a 'non-authoritarian' basis and where there is freedom to pursue a range of interests (cited in Miller and Gerard, 1979, p.309), contradict Helson's finding that the fathers of creative women consider themselves strict.

There is similarity but also divergence of findings with respect to mothers. The trend in Helson's (1999) longitudinal study of strong but bad-tempered mothers of creative women echoes, to some degree, Domino's (1979) finding of somewhat volatile mothers of those boys and girls who grow into creative teenagers. These mothers 'exhibited significantly greater interpersonal competence but coupled with a degree of indifference and detachment. They were less inhibited, more masculine, more independent and self-reliant' (p.819). Such findings suggest that the experience of growing up seeing their mothers as complex people who, in some respects, prioritised themselves above their children is potentially an important one for creative girls. However, Wallinga and Crase (1979) call into question the extent to which mothers influence, at all, the emerging creativity of their children. These authors, among other aspects they track, draw on studies which find that the creativity of mothers themselves has little bearing on the creative competence of their sons or daughters. They suggest that this is because children view their mothers as occupying an 'expressive' role (p.771) whereby she takes care of their physical and emotional needs but is not a 'person to be modeled' (ibid.). In other words, Wallinga and Crase argued, based on literature they reviewed, that children do not understand their mothers as multidimensional, complex people from which they might take direction and who might provide inspiration and a road map for their lives. This runs counter to the importance of their father in the lives of his sons and daughters, who represents an 'instrumental role' (ibid.). Unlike the mother, the father's creativity has an impact on his children's in the way that his involvement with his children tends to revolve around less conventional forms of entertainment and play than mothers. In other words, '(c)aretaking does not lend itself to exhibitions of creativity as much as does play, thus causing the mother to appear to be less creative than the fathers' (p.772), regardless of how creative the mother actually is. In addition, Wallinga and Crase (1979) reference studies by Lynn (1974) and Weinraub (1978) which find that the type of fathers who are affectionate and loving, as well as accepting and involved, 'promote competence in their children' (p.774) and that the experience of growing up with such fathers results in a 'greater tendency to exhibit creativity' (ibid.). This runs counter to the findings of strict fathers in Helson's study. Indeed, although these studies are decades old and certainly the role for women in the home has shifted dramatically from one where the mother is only the homemaker and child rearer, the picture painted in some of these studies of moderately more difficult mothers than fathers as a common dynamic in families of creative women does track with the descriptions offered by some of this study's participants.

In talking about her parents, Carole describes her mother – a music teacher – as very strict and 'regimented', with fixed ideas of appropriate behaviours. As such, there was little tolerance for expression and interests outside of those approved and proscribed by Carole's mother. Her father, however, was more 'open to things' but in general it seems to have been a typically conservative household for the 1970s in Ireland. Carole worked within the confines of what was allowed, creatively, by making dolls' houses and clothes for the dolls and decorating and arranging her own bedroom. The different personalities of her mother and father, with the former as creative herself but somewhat unyielding and perhaps not excessively affectionate and warm and the latter apparently more lenient and accepting, echoes findings outlined in Wallinga and Crase (1979) and Domino (1979) as well as aspects of Helson (1999). For Jess, growing up in a household with her mother as sole parent, the dynamic was different. She frames the performance aspect of singing in her childhood years as underscored by the resulting closeness and 'peace' that it would bring between her and her mother. In other words, her mother, with whom Jess had a loving but volatile relationship, would offer approval and express pride in Jess after a strong performance on-stage: 'I think that was in the back of my head a lot of the time as well, that kind of emotional need for validation from my mother'.

Reflecting on her childhood, it is clear that her mother played a really important role in encouraging Jess and pushing her along, but this went hand-in-hand with a 'huge anxiety' in the way her mother pitted her against others, leading to an insecurity in Jess whereby she felt like she was constantly looking over her shoulder and comparing herself to others. This resulted in her being unable to connect with others in ways where she might see them as peers from whom she could learn. Instead it was a case of being either better or worse than them. In disclosing that, 'I am very textbook in the sense that I didn't get a lot of attention as a child so I became a fucking performer you know', Jess's experience as one of a prevailing anxiety and insecurity is contrary to Miller and Gerard's (1979) assertion that emotional and economic security are vital elements of nurturing creativity in children. However, Jess's mother as a complex person does correspond with the findings from Helson's (1999) study cohort who shared the experience of having mothers who had strong and somewhat difficult personalities and who sometimes struggled with interpersonal relationships.

While Jess's father represents an absent figure in her life, Lelia's was a very important influence on her. Although she credits both her mother and father equally with encouraging an intellectual freedom, she very affectionately recalls her father as being a very open-minded kind of man whose outlook cut against the strict Catholicism of Ireland at this time. She credits this openness as resulting from his time spent working in England and being exposed to life outside the Ireland of this era: 'He was very bright and very open-hearted you know in the sense that he was very, just said "yeah of course", (but) kept an eye on us of course'. In other words, as discussed above in relation to the potential impact of warm, loving, and involved fathers on their children's creativity, Lelia's experience tallies with this in that her father provided love, safety, and security while also adopting a non-authoritarian attitude with his children. There were 'always books' in the house, she says, and her father, on an occasion when Lelia was sick in bed for a period as a child, would spend many hours reading to her. She remembers that this material tended to be books for adults rather than children's stories, and she suspects these were chosen because her father liked those books himself. But it is also indicates that her father had a respect for her intellect and for her ability to take value from good books regardless of her age or sex. Again, this has echoes of Miller and Gerard (1979), who reference Albert's (1971) findings that parents who foster a relationship with their children which is characterised by being 'open (and) adult-like' (p.309) are households where children's creativity is given room to emerge and flourish.

In short, while there are differences among this study's cohort in terms of the closeness and quality of the relationships with both parents and specifically with mothers as somewhat different to fathers, what is common across all ten women is their early exposure to art and culture. This exposure is usually underpinned by a benign indifference to their daughters' creative interests. As girls and teenagers, these women – for the most part – enjoyed loving and stable home lives where the connections and relationships between parents and daughters were not overly close or stifling. For instance, Marina reports that she was just left to get on with all the writing she was doing without being especially guided or encouraged. She says:

> There wasn't discouragement shall we say if there wasn't massive encouragement. I suppose at that age … most children … are naturally creative I think and if there are you know openings or there's some kind of mentorship I suppose that's a good thing but I suppose it's no harm either to just to be left alone you know trying things out yourself.

The following section picks up on this thread of encouragement and where the aspect of gender might figure in this.

The role of encouragement and discussions of 'gender'

While a degree of indifference characterises the approach of others towards these women's creative interests as girls and furthermore, as has been argued above, that external validation at too early an age may work to stall creativity in childhood since it undermines their freedom to take risks, there is an important role that encouragement plays in fostering creativity. For this study's cohort, there were key moments and mentors in their childhoods and adolescence when validation and encouragement were critical to their sense that they were talented. Often this encouragement occurred in schools and came from teachers who were paying attention to them, or from adults other than parents such as friends of parents. This speaks to the potentially critical influence of teachers on girls' burgeoning creativity.

Marina credits her parents with being her first mentors in the sense that the environment in which she grew up was one which actively consumed, created, and loved music and poetry and theatre: 'I suppose my parents were the first mentors really not by anything conscious they did but just by their own leading by example in a way their own love of music and writing'. Her childhood was one spent in a very rural setting with a very strong commitment and demonstration of culture in many forms: storytelling, traditional music, and ceilidh dances, as well as amateur dramatics, where she and her siblings would stage plays for neighbours written by Marina starting at the age of seven. She would go on to write, direct, and act in plays produced and put on in primary and secondary school. Something that Oonagh comments on is the 'positive feedback' and 'affirmation' she got from her parents on drawings that they would say were very good. She talks about a formative trip with her parents through Germany, Austria, and Yugoslavia in 1992 and being exposed to different cultures, youth cultures, and art, and feeling excited at the world opening up around her as a 16-year-old; such an experience is testament to her parent's willingness to encourage this exploration in Oonagh and her siblings. For Una, meanwhile, it was her sister, who went on to become an art teacher herself, who spotted Una's talent and was 'probably the biggest influencer in my life in creativity' who 'always encouraged' Una. For instance, she bought Una a portfolio when she was 16 years old with the instruction to fill it up with drawings and apply to art colleges. Una seems to have, very early on, had a natural instinct for art and shares a lovely story of drawing a picture when she was about six years old of herself outside her house and being puzzled and perplexed as to why it looked 'flat'. She remembers that by the time she was nine and drawing a rabbit, she had learnt how to improve on the drawing's dimensionality, and this time, the rabbit looked like a rabbit. Such was the likeness that this drawing resulted in Una overtaking another girl in her class to become considered the 'best at art in the class'. It seems clear that the external encouragement and recognition – from Una's sister, her classmates, and her teachers – was vital in instilling in Una a belief in her abilities. Her primary school years are characterised by being tasked with various art projects and jobs by the teachers in her school, who would then have Una 'bring them around and show other classes, which I hated because I was incredibly shy'. While this may have felt uncomfortable for Una, it no doubt was a source of pride for her and a motivation to keep going. The motivation to get stuck into art and creativity came, in part, for Annie from a teacher at school. Not academically minded in school, she got early encouragement at around eight years old from a Mrs Barber, who picked Annie out as being 'good at art'. This clearly had a big impact on Annie, who remembers, all these years later, that feeling of her talent being recognised. And she suggests that this validation was very important to her:

> If you don't have encouragement from somewhere, even from your dog, somewhere ... unless you have ... you know, I mean I'm not saying that I'm desperate for validation, it's just that I think if you have an idea for something and you're young ... and you're starting out ... unless somebody gives you a bit of feedback and gives you a bit of encouragement, it's just gonna die off because why would you do it if nobody's interested in it.

This speaks to the role that encouragement plays in the motivation to work hard at one's creative passions. Meanwhile, Amanda credits her drama teacher, Phil Dunne, with looking out for her and spurring her on, as well as other adults in her early life who were mindful that her parents were deaf and that she may, therefore, have needed a little extra assistance. Likewise, a recognition of Carole's creative skills came from two male architect friends of her father who were 'cool' and one of whom taught her watercolour. Encouragement for Carole seemed to arrive when and where it was needed. For instance, she did some work experience in an advertising agency in Dublin, arranged by her uncle, which proved to be an experience that she loved, and which resulted in her wanting to study graphic design at art college.

Liz recounts a less straightforward set of experiences characterised by both encouragement and implicit discouragement. Similar to others, she remembers early incidents of someone affirming her talent. In her case, a visitor to the house when she was about five years old commented on how good she was at drawing, something that surprised her mother and stuck with Liz later when she heard this story. Her experience of Art in school seems to have been a broadly positive one, at least early on: 'it was in the art room that I kind of came alive I suppose'. An added element was a competitive streak that saw her comparing how her drawings stacked up against her friends'. As she progressed from primary to secondary school, her sense that she was the strongest art student in the class continued. Alongside her love of art, she was keenly in love with languages, having a particular flair for French. But a poor result in her 'O' level Art exam left her 'devastated' and – even though she got very good grades in other subjects – it knocked her confidence and worried her parents about the consequences of taking Art for 'A' levels and not doing well. As a result, under pressure from parents – and silence from her teachers – she didn't pursue art in school, instead focusing on languages. It would be many years before Liz took up art again in a serious way and is a telling example of how critical the school and home environments are in recognising and nurturing creative potential in girls.

Environments and mentors that recognise and reward creativity in girls may be less common than for boys. Baer and Kaufman (2008) offer a reminder that, in societies where gender operates hierarchically, women's creative work faces judgement by others that may be directed by sexism and bias. Indeed, Miller and Gerard (1979) noted that '(g)ender differences are greatest in cultures and subcultures where gender differentiation is particularly stressed' (p.309); in other words, when boys pull way ahead of their female peers in creative accomplishment, a significant factor in this is gendered constraints imposed on girls. Thomas and Berk (1981) were interested in ascertaining how the school setting may sometimes work against the creativity of children. They pull together evidence from related studies which find that teachers prefer and prioritise 'high-IQ over highly creative pupils' (p.1153). Since the studiousness and conventional academic achievement of students considered intelligent may be not evident in creative students who think, learn, and achieve in different ways, teachers are at risk of discounting them and not accommodating or adapting their teaching styles to the needs of these students. In particular, creative girls are at higher risk of being side-lined and ignored, if not reprimanded; 'highly creative girls were viewed as particularly attention seeking and disruptive' (ibid.). This echoes Reis (2002), who warns of the detrimental effect on girls' creativity when strict gendered norms, especially relating to quietness and politeness, are imposed.

The philosophy and approach of the school can have a bearing on teaching styles and levels of freedom and flexibility afforded to students. As Thomas and Berk note, 'girls showed the greatest gain in originality in the informal schools' (p.1159) which maps onto the experience of Carole, who describes flourishing creatively and psychologically during her time at a Froebel method school, a more informal school environment which places an emphasis on self-directed and creative styles of learning. In those schools that are more rigidly structured and traditional, research has revealed (see Thomas and Berk, 1981, p.1160 for discussion), it tends to be found that teachers pull boys and girls up in different respects. With girls, teachers will castigate them for 'intellectual aspects of their school performance', while '(b)oys ... receive criticism directed primarily at nonintellectual aspects of behavior' (ibid.). For girls, this can significantly affect their 'confidence in themselves and their abilities' (ibid.). While involving a more subtle negative appraisal of her skills, Liz's experience of her teachers leading to her not pursuing Art as a Leaving Certificate subject has echoes of this research, which argues how girls' sense of their abilities can be eroded in the school environment.

While Liz was arguably let down by teachers who simply failed to pay attention to her talents, Una's school experience was characterised by a well-meaning but ultimately paternalistic and unhelpful concern over her determination to pursue a creative path. She recounts that the nuns in her school were 'horrified' at the prospect of her applying to art schools. This came less from a conservative point of view and more because 'they thought it was a terrible waste, you know they just wanted the girls, they were very progressive and wanted you know the girls out in big careers' such as engineering and so forth. They didn't consider a creative life as conducive with a 'career'. Similarly, her parents were unconvinced that it was a wise choice. Her father didn't see the point of studying art when her life would be shaped by getting married and having kids, although he did capitulate when his friend's son also went to art college and so decided to leave Una at it. Una's mother even talked to the local priest about her plans. This was motivated by a concern that art colleges were environments heavily associated with sex and drugs. It is noteworthy that it was the priest who reassured her mother that if it made Una happy and that it's what she wanted, then there was no harm. Una seems to have taken these concerns well in her stride and it didn't seem to knock her conviction in the slightest. Rather, she remained defiant with her father that she'd never marry and have kids (which she later did), and she found her mother's consultation with the local priest 'hilarious'. These experiences are similar to the fears and anxieties of Carole's parents in relation to her wanting to study at art college. But it is worth remembering that this concern or pushback from parents would not have been unusual in the 1970s and 1980s when there was little understanding or knowledge of the artistic life and of creative industries and related work. Una, amusingly and affectionately, relays that even years after she had established herself in graphic design, her mother would be amazed at the fact that Una was being approached for work and was incredibly busy: 'my mother used to say to me "gosh how are they all ringing you looking for work?" and I'm like "who knows!"'

Overall, relatively few gendered constraints were experienced by this study's cohort. Of her mother and her mother's siblings (and sisters in particular), Lelia describes them as people who – from the outside, at least – fit into conventions and expectations in the sense of getting married and having children but 'they were a very lively, independent bunch of people. You know, they got married alright, but they led somehow independent lives as well I think'. Due to a kind of self-sufficiency and independence exhibited by her mother and her female relatives, Lelia grew up with a strong, unshakeable sense of her own capabilities, abilities, and sense of independence and adventurousness: 'I ... never felt that there was any bar to anything one wanted to do'. This tallies with research (Kaplan, 2020) that women who are unconscious of or who don't dwell on their sex or on gendered norms simply get on with the work that interests them. This also speaks to the positive aspect of mothers and other women in one's early life who exude a sense of their own autonomy and who are active participants in society. In looking around at her female relatives, it was clear to Lelia as a child that 'women were quite in charge of things in a way, I mean you didn't think they couldn't be'. In other words, she absorbed and internalised this view of women as totally capable and competent in any manner of occupations, and this encouraged her to carve out her own path. So, although 'gender' was a factor in the subtle discouragement of some in terms of striving for a creative life, it has not been especially significant. This suggests that creativity in the women was not fuelled by rebelling *against* gendered norms; rather, their creativity thrived and had a chance to take root as a result of upbringings – both at home and in school – that were characterised by security and love, freedom and flexibility, but also the role of encouragement in instilling in them a confidence in their creative abilities.

References

Albert, R. S. (1971) 'Cognitive development and parental loss among the gifted, the exceptionally gifted and the creative', *Psychological Reports*, 29, pp. 19–26.

Baer, J. and Kaufman, J.C. (2008) 'Gender differences in creativity', *Journal of Creative Behavior*, 42(2), pp. 75–105. https://doi.org/10.1002/j.2162-6057.2008.tb01289.x.

Clark, M., Spence, J. and Holt, N. (2011) 'In the shoes of young adolescent girls: Understanding physical activity experiences through interpretive description', *Qualitative Research in Sport, Exercise and Health*, 3(2), pp. 193–210. https://doi.org/10.1080/2159676X.2011.572180.

Dewing, K. (1970) 'Family influences on creativity: A review and discussion', *Journal of Special Education*, 4, pp. 399–404.

Domino, G. (1979) 'Creativity and the home environment', *Gifted Child Quarterly*, 23(4), pp. 818–828. https://doi.org/10.1177/001698627902300414.

Foster, F.P. (1968) 'The human relationships of creative individuals', *Journal of Creative Behavior*, 2(2), pp. 111–118.

Helson, R. (1999) 'A longitudinal study of creative personality in women', *Creativity Research Journal*, 12(2), pp. 89–101. https://doi.org/10.1207/s15326934crj1202 _2.

Kaplan, J. (2020) *The genius of women: From overlooked to changing the world.* Dutton: Penguin Random House.

Koppman, S. (2016) 'Different like me: Why cultural omnivores get creative jobs', *Administrative Science Quarterly*, 61(2), pp. 291–331. https://doi.org/10.1177 /0001839215616840.

Latorre Román, P.Á., Pinillos, F.G., Pantoja Vallejo, A. and Berrios Aguayo, B. (2017) 'Creativity and physical fitness in primary school-aged children', *Pediatrics International: Official Journal of the Japan Pediatric Society*, 59(11), pp. 1194–1199. https://doi.org/10.1111/ped.13391.

Lubart, T. and Guignard, J.H. (2004) 'The generality-specificity of creativity: A multivariate approach', in Sternberg, R.J., Grigorenko, E.L. and Singer, J.L. (eds.) *Creativity: From potential to realization.* Washington, DC: American Psychological Association, pp. 43–56.

Lynn, D. B. (1974) *The father: His role in child development.* Monterey, CA.: Brooks/Cole.

Miller, B.C. and Gerard, D. (1979) 'Family influences on the development of creativity in children: An integrative review', *The Family Coordinator*, 28(3), pp. 295–312. https://doi.org/10.2307/581942.

Reis, S.M. (2002) 'Toward a theory of creativity in diverse creative women', *Creativity Research Journal*, 14(3–4), pp. 305–316. https://doi.org/10.1207/ S15326934CRJ1434_2.

Selby, E.C., Shaw, E.J. and Houtz, J.C. (2005) 'The creative personality', *Gifted Child Quarterly*, 49(4), pp. 300–314. https://doi.org/10.1177/001698620504900404.

Thomas, N.G. and Berk, L.E. (1981) 'Effects of school environments on the development of young children's creativity', *Child Development*, 52(4), pp. 1153–1162. https://doi.org/10.2307/1129501.

Wallinga, C.R. and Crase, S.J. (1979) 'Parental influence on creativity of fifth grade children', *Gifted Child Quarterly*, 23(4), pp. 768–777. https://doi.org/10.1177 /001698627902300408.

Weinraub, M. (1978) 'Fatherhood: The myth of the second class parent', in Stevens, J.H. Jr. and Matthew, M. (eds.) *Mother/child father/child relationships.* Washington, D.C.: National Association for the Education of Young Children, pp. 109–133.

3 Further education and early career

Encouragement as vital to building creative confidence

Emerging from adolescence into the years of their young adulthood and, later, the phase of early career, the women faced some challenges but in large part, these years are ones of honing a craft and of support and mentorship from influential people in their lives. The entry into further education and training, that most of the women took, is instrumental is providing a physical as well as a cognitive creative space in which they could try their hand working at a range of practices related to their preferred creative fields. This has proven to be critical at enabling them to build a confidence in their abilities as well as to benefit from both mentors and peers; something that offered both encouragement and constructive critique. Building a career for themselves was, in general, not a clear or straight path. Rather, for many there was an open-minded approach to opportunities that presented themselves, with this cohort taking things as they came and making the most of such chances when they could.

Learning and growing through further education and training

Third-level or further educational opportunities are found to be absolutely critical to all the interviewees. The time at college or training afforded many of these women the time, space, and opportunity to try their hand at a range of creative practices until they figured out what interested them and where their strengths lay. Although Una Healy didn't receive an offer of a place at NCAD (National College of Art and Design) and was 'heartbroken', a foundational course in art and design at what is now IADT (Dún Laoghaire Institute of Art, Design and Technology) allowed her to have a go at a wide range of creative practices. During this year, the students did woodwork, sculpture, jewellery, and illustration. It was the illustration, typography, and graphic design work that Una really took to:

> I knew I wasn't going to be a painter, I didn't have the talent to be a painter or sculptor … but it was the graphic design that always appealed

DOI: 10.4324/9781003082750-3

to me, that it was problem-solving and you had to come up with some solution that would work and I liked that.

She credits her graphic design teacher during this foundation course with opening up the world of design to her. This year was then followed by three years of Visual Communications studies. Throughout her college years, she would try other mediums, but graphic design and illustration was what she continued to specialise in. This aspect of turning her hand to a number of creative practices is one shared by Annie West. Like Una, Annie also studied at Dún Laoghaire college. She describes, in the lead up to leaving secondary school, spending 'a very big weekend putting a portfolio together, copying everything and tracing, and just generally throwing stuff into a portfolio; lying, basically!' In all likelihood, she is downplaying the quality of the portfolio but, in any case, she considers the principal of Dún Laoghaire art college at the time as 'taking pity' on her in accepting her onto the foundation course. This represents an important lifeline for her at a crunch time when she is on the cusp of leaving school and is getting little to no guidance or direction from school or at home from her parents.

Her time at Dún Laoghaire is one where she understands herself as something of an outsider, as not fitting in with the 'arty' crowd in their 'floaty outfits'. She frames herself as not as accomplished as her classmates, but this acknowledgement belies a strongly apparent inner confidence in herself, her creative abilities and – critically – her appetite to learn and to work hard. There is evidence too of an anti-establishment streak during these years at college. This is arguably borne of not feeling 'as good as' others and therefore different but is also testament to her independent-mindedness. She rails against the conventions and expectations of what a creative type at art college *should* be: 'I'll do this my way', she promised herself. She credits her connection or bond with a few of her lecturers as her saving grace in sticking it out at Dún Laoghaire:

> If I hadn't got the support and encouragement that I did get from the tutors that I had, which I was very lucky to have, I don't think I would have lasted as far as graduation and I certainly wouldn't have continued with it.

Through their mentorship, she was exposed to a range of different practices and skills. For instance, her teacher in the screen-printing workshop was 'very encouraging' of Annie's initiation into this skill. Such encouragement cannot be underestimated. As the hugely successful musical artist Tori Amos notes in an interview in the *New Yorker*, 'Somebody might have ability ... but if that isn't nurtured ... then it can get stunted' (Petrusich, 2020, para. 8). For Annie, her creativity is certainly nurtured at Dún Laoghaire and much faith is poured into her abilities. At a later point, she is given the choice of animation or production design for TV. She chooses production design because of a perception of animation as too nerdy and boring. This is surprising given her later work is in the sphere of animation, but it would result in her picking up a wide array of skills in the higher education setting, which she would later draw on during her roles in television and film production. Alongside her determination to succeed through hard work, she recognises the chance and happenstance nature of her years in college and credits this fact – and the input of mentors – with directing her to a path that would work out for her after graduation and would, crucially, open doors. Indeed, as Selby, Shaw, and Houtz (2005) note, it is teachers and instructors who are best placed to adapt teaching styles to creative students so they can approach tasks in ways that best suit their aptitudes. Annie seems to have benefitted from having such lecturers and tutors in her life.

Research suggests that the experience of having mentors and those in their lives who are supportive is crucial for creative women. Reis (2002) finds in her study that 'despite negative formal educational experiences, these creative artists generally had supportive families and the benefit of at least one influential mentor in their lives' (p.308), and she notes that women will seek out 'role models' in their childhoods, adolescence, or early career and often credit these people with their eventual creative successes. Contrary to Reis's cohort, the women of this study did not report negative educational experiences. Rather, it has been because of the attention and affirmation of instructors, lecturers, and peers, as well as a generally positive environment during further education, that these women would stick to the creative path. During Carole Pollard's years at the School of Architecture at Bolton Street, Dublin Institute of Technology, a very mixed and sometimes negative and discouraging experience would eventually be turned around, thanks to the explicit support of some teaching staff. After the excitement of starting college wore off, her first- and second-year studies of architecture were incredibly tough. She had to face instances of very overt and aggressive sexism. She, and other female students, experienced groping and wolf-whistling in the corridors of Bolton Street, and she recalls on one occasion all the girls in the class of one male teacher were failed. Carole remembers him patronisingly tell her that her handwriting was lovely, and she should consider working in an architect's office and 'keeping it tidy'. She ended up having to repeat her second year, but by third year she was no longer sure if the architecture field was for her. She dropped out and worked in London for a stint at an architect's office, which reignited her interest, and so she returned to Bolton Street to finish her studies. Some encouragement at this time was a major factor in her thriving. Specifically, a male lecturer 'took me under his wing a lot' and she worked part-time in his practice. By her fourth and fifth year, there was some staff turnover and, with more women lecturers in the mix, the atmosphere changed significantly and substantially improved.

This more positive and constructive environment, with staff demonstrating a faith in her abilities, was critical to Carole finishing her architecture degree. Lisa Mulcahy similarly tells of a highly positive and encouraging college experience. With five siblings ahead of her, by the time she was leaving school and picking courses for college, she and her sister just elder to her – both more artistic than the others in the family – were not under the same pressure as their older siblings to choose areas of study directed by their father. Consequently, having been 'always interested in television', she applied for and got a place on a Media Studies course. She went on to study Media Studies in the early 1980s at what became the Dublin Institute of Technology. The course involved filmmaking, predominantly. She remembers this as a fantastic time. There were equal places reserved for male and female students, resulting in a very healthy balance and dynamic between the sexes. As part of the European Social Fund, students were paid to study, so she didn't have financial worries. Instead, she and her classmates simply began their training in how to go about making films: 'we learnt how to edit them and do the sound and do the props and that's what we did'. In other words, Lisa and her classmates enjoyed a productive, creative, and fruitful education, one that enabled experimentation and skill-building.

Fostering women's talents and interests in creative practice are vital to ensuring that their creative potential is nurtured and is converted into creative achievement. To revisit the question posed in the opening chapter as to why men have excelled in the creative fields in far higher numbers than women, the aspects of education, support, and patronage play a hugely significant role. Korsmeyer (2004) notes that '(n)o matter what gifts nature may bestow on artists, they must be trained; without education genius is merely a potential' (p.59). The fact remains, however, that education and instruction has historically been withheld from women. As previously discussed, withholding of creative training for women and girls has been justified – especially in patriarchal societies – by reference to sexist and essentialist claims of women's intellectual inferiority. Given the supposed inability of the female sex to learn pursuits of a cognitively and creatively complex nature, it would amount to a waste of everyone's time to try to teach her skills that she is, through no fault of her own, incapable of mastering. In addition to biological deterministic beliefs about women's inferiority, the social mores of different periods also served to exclude women from fully flexing their creative muscles. In other words, since a woman's virtue and respectability were often uppermost in the qualities she should exhibit, the kind of worldliness and 'breadth of experience' (Korsmeyer, 2004, p.61) that was considered a requirement in order to create great works of art and literature were simply outside the sphere of experience for women. Consequently, as Korsmeyer notes, in some respects the problem is not always that women are precluded from creative pursuits, but that their work – when they did produce something for consumption – was automatically judged as having a 'restricted scope and narrow vision, insuring that women's efforts will be counted as minor' (ibid.). Cameron (2018) also touches on this in pointing out that the art world and the creative fields do not apply equal standards when reviewing and judging men and women's work. Rather, there is an assumption that underpins women's creative outputs which is that it's necessarily 'minor' as well as 'mediocre, derivative, trivial, sentimental, "light". It has, in other words, the same negative qualities that are often attributed to women themselves' (p.110). Chadwick (1990) offers a stark example of this double standard in action by reference to a sexist review of a 1946 New York exhibition by painter Louise Nevelson by one male critic who wrote 'We learned the artist was a woman, in time to check our enthusiasm ... Had it been otherwise, we might have hailed these sculptural expressions as by surely a great figure among the moderns' (cited in Chadwick, 1990, p.308). Such a remarkable statement is clear evidence that the sex of the creator can predetermine how seriously, or not – as the case may be for women – to approach a review of the work. These few sentences also reveal an anxiety about the reviewer's close brush with public humiliation, as if he would have felt duped, hoodwinked, or embarrassed if her sex had not been known to him and he had publicly commended her work. Of course, this open admission of bias on the basis of sex was not unusual, either then, in the decades after, or indeed, centuries before. The 19th-century German philosopher Schopenhauer proclaimed, in relation to women, that

> The most distinguished intellects among the whole sex have never managed to produce a single achievement in the fine arts that is really great, genuine, and original; or given to the world any work of permanent value in any sphere.
>
> (cited in Korsmeyer, 2004, p.67)

Considering that these sentiments were widespread, it is no surprise that the effect that this belief-system had on women's creative education was devastating. Nochlin (1971) takes up this subject in seeking to explain why '(t)here *are* no women equivalents for Michelangelo or Rembrandt, Delacroix' (p.196–197). While a common narrative around women's historic involvement in art and creative practice often focuses on rediscovering and reclaiming women who have been ignored, underappreciated, or forgotten over time, Nochlin takes a different approach, which is to point out that there haven't been great women artists included in the category of the 'master' painters. She suggests that the lack of encouragement, patronage, and support given to women is to blame for their relative absence in creative and artistic endeavour, and that they didn't have the 'good fortune to be born white, preferably middle class and, above all, male' (p.197). She goes on to argue that '(t)he fault lies not in our stars, hormones, our menstrual cycles, or our empty internal spaces, but in our institutions and our education' (p.197) and that it is a testament to women's creative drive that so many, relatively speaking, did make successful creative lives for themselves. Nochlin is insistent that women's absence from creative fields has to account for this aspect of training, since the journey to creative excellence and accomplishment is a long one that starts in childhood and requires tutelage and support along the way. Many years later, Lubart and Guignard (2004) would also maintain that outside influence, in the forms of support, encouragement, and rewards constitute just one aspect or component of creativity, along with 'domain-relevant skills (which) include knowledge, technical skills, and special talents relevant to the task domain' (p.45) as well as internally derived characteristics such as 'persistence and sustained attention to a task' (ibid.). These factors all speak to a desirable combination of innate skill, internal or psychological qualities or traits associated with hard work and determination, opportunities for training and skills acquisition, as well as external encouragement and support for one's creative work.

These aspects of positive feedback and encouragement, as well as the contention that self-perception of one's creative ability as critical is evident in the findings of this study. Amanda Coogan, for instance, started out with an academic background in art. She pursued a diploma in painting from Limerick and later a sculpture degree from NCAD before a move into performance art. She was determined to train with the best and set out to work under the inimitable Serbian performance artist, Marina Abramović. At this pre-internet time, Amanda had to write letters to colleges across Germany to try to track Abramović down and find out where she taught. She credits IMMA (The Irish Museum of Modern Art) with being helpful and supportive enough in reaching out to Abramović on Amanda's behalf. This led to Amanda sending Abramović her portfolio and then to being invited to join Abramović's class at an art college in Germany. The two-year experience in Germany was a massively important and formative experience for Amanda and cemented the conviction that this form of artistic practice would be her life's creative work.

Jess Kavanagh also touches on the subject of support and encouragement. Having lost her mother just before she turned 21 years of age, she found herself very much alone and without the network of family enjoyed by most of her peers. But support from college classmates and friends enabled her to juggle it all and to do well in her studies. At age 24, she got a scholarship to study music in London. The whole experience and atmosphere of studying in London and the vibrant, dynamic, and exciting aspect of living in Brixton were undermined somewhat by not quite managing to find her 'tribe' with whom to make music. As a result, she came back to Dublin to join up with some friends in bands. But after trying out some things, by the age of 26 or 27 she was still 'a bit lost'. Around this time, she started working with the male friends with whom she would later form a band, and she joined the weekly Wednesday night jam sessions at Dame Lane, a time that seems to have been very creatively rewarding for her and one which she suggests was a uniquely enriching and interesting time in the Irish music scene for its multicultural inclusion and collaboration. Her recollections of this period are notable for the atmosphere of teaching, learning, and growing from each other in the music scene at the time.

Personal and creative growth during their college years are evident in the conversations with both Oonagh Kearney and Lelia Doolan. Oonagh studied Philosophy and English at University College Cork. While she credits philosophy with teaching her an ability to think critically, it was the extracurricular time spent involved in putting on and producing plays at college which ignited an interest in theatre that hadn't necessarily been there in secondary school. This experience of playwrighting would lead her to undertaking an MPhil in Theatre at Trinity College Dublin, after which she returned to Cork with a stronger sense of belonging to the theatre and arts scene in the city. For Lelia, in her years at University College Dublin studying French, she was more invested with the drama society (Dram Soc) than with her studies. She had been interested in theatre ever since her father would bring her to opera and pantomimes when she was young. Her involvement with the Dram Soc during these years included acting in and producing many stage productions. There is a great degree of activity and experimentation at this time – of trying things out: 'it was heady times; I mean, it was enjoyable'. After spending a summer in Kilkee, Co. Clare with a crowd from the theatre set, she went to Berlin to study theatre under the German theatre playwright and director Bertolt Brecht. Coming back from Berlin, she continued to pursue the theatre as an occupation, although with little conscious consideration of 'making a living' through it. At this point, she was predominantly acting in the plays that were staged, some with high-profile directors and actors. But she was also doing some of the PR and publicity for these productions, as well as writing a column for a local paper in Dún Laoghaire. She remembers some of the theatre productions she was involved in as controversial.

On being asked if the prevailing attitudes around conservatism and shame regarding subjects pertaining to sex were a worry to her given her involvement in staging some plays that dealt with these themes, she says 'no I never worried about it, I never thought about it'. Partly, she thinks, this was due to simply being a bit blinkered. In other words, she was enjoying herself too much to give much thought to how the work was received by a public far more socially conservative than she and her friends. She seems to have been insulated from and oblivious to the 'gloomy and rather cruel' 1950s and early 1960s Ireland in which she was living and working. But whatever about her insulation from the worst of the conservatism in Ireland, her thriving in the creative space of the theatre at this time is, in part, as a result of the consistent encouragement and positive feedback she got from those around her who pushed her along.

This topic of the potential benefits of varying types of feedback in developing the best approach to teaching creativity to students is one that Mattern, Child, Vanhorn, and Gronewold (2013) sought to investigate. They surveyed over 500 students, and their findings show that, contrary to their hypothesis that positive feedback would be positively correlated to creative output, there was some indication that students who received negative feedback showed evidence of working harder in response to this kind of evaluation. However, the major caveat of their study is that the results are based on only one exercise. Perhaps more compelling is the literature that their study draws on which shows that one's creative confidence and sense of one's own creative abilities is 'built over time through successes or failures we have experienced (Seligman and Csikszentmihalyi, 2000). If those experiences have been largely positive, one develops confidence in his or her creative ability' (Mattern et al., 2013, p.16). This points to the potential detrimental effect of negative feedback over time, which can dent the confidence of the student. The authors go on to note that 'creativity can be a self-fulfilling prophecy' (ibid.) and that 'Confidence-destroying experiences can lead to lower self-perceptions of creativity, and confidence-building experiences can have the opposite effect' (ibid.). Though there is no sex-disaggregated data or corresponding discussion of gender in this study, there is a very real risk that, in societies and settings were sexism and gendered norms are strongly in place, that girls and women are more likely to be subjected to confidence-destroying experiences, since some research has indicated that teachers and instructors react more negatively to creative girls displaying traits of creativity where they are assumed to be disruptive and trouble-making (Thomas and Berk, 1981). The experience of this study's cohort receiving consistently encouraging and positive feedback over time from key mentors in their lives perhaps plays an important role in building a confidence and in providing a solid foundation on which they could anchor a faith in their own creative abilities.

Kaplan (2020) also touches on the common themes in the lives of women who far exceed the achievements of their peers. One such theme is that '(g)enius needs to be nurtured' (p.302). In other words, for talented women to make it, they need at least one cheerleader who instils in them a belief in their abilities. This attests to the care and attention that needs to be given to creative girls as they grow through adolescence and early adulthood. For those women who succeed in carving out a creative life and career for themselves, they share a 'common story', as Brooks and Daniluk (1998) suggest. The story hits the same plot points, which begin with 'creative exploration and identity struggles in childhood and adolescence' (p.255) and then sees the young women in a process of working out what direction to take their creative talents. Later, there are challenges of establishing careers and practices alongside other demands of their lives. And the story culminates in a 'consolidation of their identities as artists and in their feelings of satisfaction with the lives and careers they had created for themselves' (ibid.).

There is much here that tallies with the lives and career trajectories of this study's cohort and the following section – and chapters – set this out. In the meantime, the early career years of these women reveal an energy and appetite for hard work and a willingness to make significant sacrifices to follow one's creative path. Marina Carr, for instance, may not have set out to 'make it' as a playwright, nor did she give much thought to the feasibility of being able to make a living from writing. Instead, through a dogged and sustained approach to writing, she gradually started being able to make ends meet in a cumulative fashion, where one play would get accepted by theatres and then a commission would come along. Although funds remained very tight, she says,

> that didn't bother me as a young woman, I kind of liked that freedom and that hand to mouth existence but I suppose when you're young you do you know, you don't have to be thinking of mortgages and school fees and you know all that kind of stuff.

These can-do and work-hard attitudes are common across all the women interviewed for the study.

Early career: setbacks and opportunities

These years after college and further education, when their working lives are becoming established, are ones that see them grow in confidence as they hone their chosen crafts and develop a greater sense of their creative capabilities. What is critical to this is the faith that others, such as industry colleagues and bosses, demonstrated in their abilities and ideas. Lelia's early career is quite remarkable for the degree to which she was entrusted with responsibilities early on. After a tour of *The Playboy* around London, she came back to Ireland and got together enough money to head off to the Aran Islands for a few months to learn Irish; when she returned to Dublin, television was taking off, and in 1960 RTÉ was established. She 'was encouraged [by family] to apply for a job as a director-producer'. This testifies to the support and faith of family, friends, and mentors as crucial at pivotal moments in the life of women pursuing artistic and creative work. She had a male mentor who ran the *South Dublin Post*, for which Lelia wrote, who would encourage her to 'keep on writing'. She talks about a kind of social and political awakening happening during those early years with RTÉ when she was producing programmes for the station. An especially important experience comes in the form of a training trip to the US with broadcaster CBS on producing news programmes where she is exposed to the social, cultural, and political events of the day, such as the Harlem riots and the early years of the civil rights movement. This stoked her interest in a world wider than her theatre set.

Her experience at RTÉ indicates that, in giving the job of producer-director to a woman, it was an organisation more progressive than the country at the time. And, in funding a three-month trip to the US for her, this faith was backed up with investment in her and her skillset. Of particular note is the influence and mentorship of Gunnar Rugheimer, RTÉ controller of programmes at the time, who strongly encouraged Lelia to take ownership of her role, to be ambitious and problem-solving, and to take risks: 'he became a mentor in the sense that he would say "Lelia you better do something about this", or "what do you think of doing this or will you do that?" and so I began to do [so]'. He entrusted her with directing RTÉ's flagship soap *The Riordans*. After *The Riordans*, Lelia created the *Seven Days* current affairs programme and again took risks in calling to account those in power. On one occasion, renowned American broadcast journalist Walter Cronkite contributed to a package which was broadcast on the programme about the importance of an independent public service broadcaster. This was a direct response, she says, to a provocative statement issued by then-Taoiseach Seán Lemass, in which he stated that public broadcasting was 'an arm of public policy', to which she and colleagues fundamentally and for obvious reasons disagreed and decided to take some kind of stand on. This really points at a kind of bravery, fearlessness, and lack of reverence or bowing down to those in power, something Lelia carries through her whole life. All of this was enabled in the early years of her career in broadcasting and programme-making.

Among other opportunities that opened up for her, Annie also credits RTÉ with providing a chance for her to hone her skills. She got lucky for the fact that she was the only person in Dún Laoghaire college taking production design, so she had the sole benefit of Michael Grogan's tutelage and it meant she secured part-time work in RTÉ where, she says, she worked incredibly hard. Of this job, she says, 'I kind of jumped into that fully and just embraced the whole thing and went in there and I worked my backside off, I had to'. She notes at least four of her tutors in college were incredibly encouraging and gave her a confidence in her aptitude for production design. As she puts it, 'they'd all sort of gone "you're pretty good at this ...", and things started to unfold in my brain'. The unfurling of ideas in her brain were strongly supported by those she worked with in RTÉ, meaning that the transition from college to a career in production and graphic design is characterised by creative freedom and faith in her, whereby she remembers this time as one where she'd

> come up with these crazy ideas for things and then because I had the idea, now I have to go and do it! But because I had somebody like Nick who said 'right, well let's do that' rather than having somebody say 'oh for god's sake, that's a stupid idea'.

In other words, she encountered really important confidence-building experiences that spurred her on. This provided crucial motivation for her to work incredibly hard, and she acknowledges that she felt she had to work 'ten times harder than everybody else because some people were just naturally talented at drawing but they're also very lazy whereas I was technically good at things but had to work ten times harder just to get to that'.

The move into film for Oonagh echoes the experiences of Lelia and Annie in that there are industry people and those in positions of power who take a chance on them and believe in their abilities. In Oonagh's case, this is reflected in an opportunity provided by Ken Loach to work on his 2006 film *The Wind That Shakes the Barley* and she became his casting director on that film. She credits Loach with being a really influential and important mentor to her in her early foray into the film industry:

> He was a key mentor along the road because he's so vastly experienced. He knew exactly what he was doing, he was literally holding my hand and trusting me. Like, no one gave me more responsibility ever in a film since as Ken Loach did when I had not worked on a single film.

This experience was one of huge enjoyment and was so rewarding for Oonagh that it turned her attention to the idea of studying film and becoming a filmmaker. The beginning of that journey started in London at the National Film and Television School, and she stayed there for a decade 'learning (her) craft'.

For Liz O'Kane, a pivotal moment comes when she is encouraged by a teacher during an interior design course at Liberties College in Dublin to do a work placement at a foundry:

> One of the ceramics teachers recognised – more than I recognised myself – that I had really strong sculptural leaning and she suggested that I do a college placement in a foundry … she was good enough to ring around a number of the Dublin foundries to see if anyone would take in a student on a work placement and I ended up working for a fortnight with Cast Foundry and Leo Higgins, the manager there, took me under his wing. He was amazing, he would be a person I would say who's being a really strong mentor to me.

At the point when Liz took up the course at Liberties College, she had largely stopped practising art, so this experience and the direction and encouragement given by teachers and instructors were hugely important in her eventual, very successful, career in sculpture. The positive impact on her confidence from her mastering of a new skill are clear in how she talks about the practice of sculpture. She says, 'I just fell in love with it … I felt more alive than I probably ever had before in any other setting'. This speaks to the critical role of confidence-building experiences in creativity and creative risk-taking and accomplishment, as discussed previously. Liz's love for the practice of sculpture was something she dreamed of turning into a living but, in the early stages, this seemed unrealistic. However, she did do just that, and notes that 'it was only something that came around very gradually and always by accident and one thing would lead to another or one meeting or one commission would lead to another'. Again, what Liz's career trajectory demonstrates is that support and patronage, financial and otherwise, provide enough incentive for creative artists and practitioners to keep going.

Getting opportunities to practice one's craft, to make a start on one's career, and to be paid for work done are issues garnering much attention for feminists and advocacy groups focused on women in the CCIs. The Arts Council of Ireland, for instance, has been publishing reports tracking the issue of gender and making available statistics that breakdown applications and awards by the sex of the applicant. The 2019 round of awards shows that while male applicants, making up 39% of applications, requested greater amounts of funding than the women and indeed generally received more money than the female applicants, women did win 63% of the awards (Arts Council, 2020). This indicates a very positive picture with regards to women creatives in Ireland receiving state-backed financial support for their work and projects. This trend is somewhat less pronounced for the 2020 scheme, with women making up 55% of the applicants and 59% of the awardees. Nevertheless, as noted by the Arts Council (2021), women 'are slightly over-represented compared to population statistics in the 2016 Census' (p.6). As such, these statistics represent a very healthy balance between male and female creatives and artists seeking and securing funding for their creative practices in Ireland.

The structured and transparent nature of these kinds of funding schemes can be especially important for women in their early career in the creative sphere since there has been a well-documented trend or issue with opportunities passing from men to other men. Wing-Fai, Gill, and Randle (2015) refer to 'reputation economies' in relation to the film and TV industries which sees 'people ... hired on the soft judgements of insiders about whether they are trustworthy, reliable and good to work with' (p.56). The authors point out that the 'informal, word of mouth nature' (p.56) of hiring and recruitment, especially with respect to freelance roles in these creative industries, means that the aspect of networking and having firm contacts who are already established in these areas is critical to being in with a chance of 'getting in' and 'getting on', as they put it. For women, and indeed people from backgrounds not typically involved in creative and cultural work, there can be challenges and barriers which mean it may be more difficult to spend time, outside work hours, socialising and networking with the right people. Conor, Gill, and Taylor (2015) also point out that in the CCIs, 'reputation becomes a key commodity, and networking and maintaining contacts a key activity for nurturing it' (p.10) They suggest that increasing awareness of this serves to highlight the fact that 'women fare better in settings in which there is both greater formality to the hiring process and greater transparency' (p.11).

The aspect of 'trust' is raised by Jones and Pringle (2015) and they note that 'networking must focus on trustworthy recruits who will fit in immediately and are seen as competent' (p.39). Milestone (2015) also attests to this. In talking to hiring managers and other gatekeepers in the cultural industries about their approach to hiring and recruitment, they often reveal that the training, formal qualifications, and prior experience of candidates take a back seat to the criteria of having been recommended for a role. In other words, Milestone found that the issue 'of "fitting in" was a recurrent theme in the majority of companies that were interviewed and seems to be a euphemism for recruiting "people like us". This attitude makes the prospect of a diverse workforce unattainable' (p.507). This calls to mind Koppman's (2016) research, her concept of cultural omnivorousness and her contention that creative jobs are at risk of going to those who share similarities and shared creative tastes with those in gatekeeper and hiring positions. As such, there are considerable potential challenges for women in getting selected for roles that rely so heavily on a system of personal vouching and where the mostly male hiring managers and gatekeepers may have a preference for others who are like them.

The experiences of this study's cohort do not generally track with the findings of these studies as they pertain to recruitment and hiring in more established creative organisations, or in being selected for freelance or project roles. Instead, even though these women largely operated in an unstructured, freelance space and therefore could have found themselves more vulnerable to being shut out, squeezed out, or exploited, they describe getting opportunities – often from male mentors and champions – all along in their career. However, the issue of slightly different kinds of setbacks and challenges in the early career phase was raised by several interviewees. Although the issue of exploitation and overt sexism is one that is, thankfully, not typical in the early career accounts of these women, some interviewees noted some challenges and difficulties. For instance, on the process of writing, the idea of a girl writing plays was something Marina grew up thinking was 'really natural'. This is thanks to the freedom that characterised her childhood and later the encouragement from her father who enabled Marina and her siblings to figure out who they were and what they wanted to do. Consequently, it came as a shock when, early on, she was scrutinised and criticised by those in the culture and theatre communities who, in a way that can be considered derogatory, would describe her as a 'female playwright' by way of trying to pigeonhole her. She considers such a qualifier as serving as a reminder that her work is simply just 'about women'. However, she was and remains defiant that this does not represent her work and in fact diminishes what she does:

> I use the whole canvas as I feel I have the right to do but I think there is something out there in the – what shall we call it – the patriarchal structure that likes to … it's like the way they used to say about women poets you know 'oh they write in the first person', you know, 'it's all confessional'. It was a way to kind of give them a little rap on the knuckles you know or call them 'poetesses' the same way I was a 'female playwright' and that I could write about women and it was like that's as much of the canvas as you are permitted and whereas I've always written thinking I was writing the whole canvas so … that still is a challenge I think for both myself and for others I see as well working.

In other words, Marina has felt the sharp end of sexism in how her work was sometimes diminished and considered less serious or universally appealing simply because she is a woman writing plays. This, of course, is reminiscent of the essentialist worldviews and opinions held by some who would posit that women are incapable of creating great art.

Carole also talks about some rocky roads with respect to her early career years. After graduation, she took up a role with a big firm but didn't enjoy the work, which she found was too repetitive and routinised, with the workday too structured to suit her. She remembers, 'you had to be in at 9, the bell rang for tea break in the morning, you had lunch from 1 til 2 … the bell rang for tea break in the afternoon and then you couldn't leave til 6'. She also notes that the experience of having a child early in her career proved very difficult:

> I had a huge enthusiasm and a huge energy at that stage in my life … and then to have a baby and for all of that to kind of fall back on itself in a way, yeah it was difficult and a very lonely few years cos I had my second child 14 months later, so I had two small babies, I was working from the box room in the house that we lived in but this one client who … I continued to do work for, she was a good support.

Again, as described by Carole, at a key moment in her life and career when she may have stepped away entirely from the field of architecture, the support from one client represented a lifeline at a time where she was isolated and 'lonely'.

Jess recalls more obviously sexist and unpleasant experiences. In her mid-to-late 20s, a high-profile male artist saw her talent and invited her to join him and his band as a back-up singer. Consequently, she went out on tour with them for a period. This was clearly a mixed experience for her, with some of the male musicians in the band acting in ways that were 'sexist' and 'homophobic'. On another experience touring with a band and supporting performers, Jess discusses the strategies she had to learn in dealing with men on the tour bus espousing views she found sexist and homophobic:

> There was nowhere to escape and so … you would have to learn very quickly to either put up with it or find ways to stand up for yourself that didn't come across as combative, and that is unfortunately something you would have to learn as a touring female musician and … the first time I came across it I was combative immediately, I was just like you know I wanted to humiliate him because I felt he deserved to be humiliated for using such terms, it didn't work and at the end of the day the onus or the attention would come back on me as the one who is being aggressive and that stereotype then would just be amplified so that was

very disheartening, it was very disheartening to have that as my first experience and then for my second experience to be if not worse.

She identifies, not so much a generational issue, but a class issue in the sexism and homophobia she witnessed. These were middle-class guys she worked with in bands, and she suggests they exhibited a kind of arrogance and superiority and were patronising and 'condescending' to female band-mates. Jess also a saw in them a sense that, because they were well-educated, they believed that their behaviours couldn't be considered sexist.

As Holt and Lapenta (2010) have noted, much research in the past few decades have sought to shine a spotlight on the issue of exploitation in the creative industries. They suggest that because of the 'strong positive associations with creative work' (p.223), this can belie the potential for abuse, harassment, and taking advantage of workers who operate under precarious conditions given that the nature of labour in the CCIs is often unregulated freelance and project work. The tallies with Conor, Gill, and Taylor's (2015) argument that, in pointing out inequalities and issues of poor representation in the CCIs, scholars must grapple with the 'enduring and powerful' (p.10) perception of the creative and cultural sphere as one founded on principles of fairness, inclusion, and equality.

Alongside both opportunities and setbacks, these early career years mark an important transition towards a more established creative identity and a conviction in our featured artists' and creatives' skills and abilities. On the question of what sustained her in her belief that a career in music would work out, Jess says:

> I thought I was the best singer, like 100%. I was completely confident in a way which was detrimental because I couldn't take criticism and … if it didn't fit my sense of self and sense of identity I would reject it and couldn't take it, but the positive side of that was that during difficult times I was just 100% completely confident that I could power through with my voice and that any person who would hear me sing would definitely give me a job.

In other words, her self-belief was both a strongly held conviction in her talent but also a form of self-defence in the sense that not admitting to weaknesses protected her sense of herself. She puts this confidence down to something internal rather external; it didn't form from others around her telling her she was brilliant, but rather, she believes, she always felt that way. For Lisa, there's a degree of falling into doing something that she found she loved and was good at. In other words, she didn't really set out to work in film and TV and actually had no idea what those industries or the work involved since there were no family members or family friends who worked in this field by way of reference. She seems to have thrived during the college experience and secured a job in film and editing before she left. Similarly, for Una, there is much satisfaction expressed in her career. Immediately after graduating college, a stint at an animation company in Dublin where she spent days 'painting bubbles' for a scene on *An American Tail* and later joining another company 'setting up the backgrounds for the animation' left her 'really bored' so she moved to London where she ended up doing very well in the graphic design industry and stayed for three years.

The ways in which these women discuss the early years in their chosen creative fields, it's clear that there is a simultaneous exploration of their craft, their talents, and themselves alongside one another. Brooks and Daniluk (1998) centre this topic of 'women artists' creative identity development' (p.256) and note that their findings track with other scholars who report that creative women typically suffer at the beginning stages of their career as a result of 'lack of familial and social support for art as a "legitimate" career and by the absence of female role models and mentors in the arts' (p.255). And they contend that 'creative identity development was a long, difficult, and nonlinear process, often involving intense feelings of illegitimacy, self-doubt, guilt, and resentment' (p.256). Some of these themes of guilt and resentment will be picked up in the next chapters, but what resonates with this study is the assertion that the establishment of a creative identity is a long and complex process. For some interviewees however, most notably Amanda, a creative sense of self was present from a very young age. Amanda seems to have always had a determination to carve out a creative life for herself. She has very consciously, from young adulthood and in the initial years of her performance art practice, been aware that she would have to live 'frugally' and forego the security of permanent jobs and the expectations of houses and cars and so forth in order to work her life around practising as an artist. In part this meant not being seduced by taking on 'money work', and, specifically for Amanda, not getting sucked into gradually doing more and more sign language interpreter work which would have cut into the time and energy required to continue with her practice. Reiger's (1983) longitudinal study into women given the designation of 'high' or 'low' creatives and what might distinguish one group from another indicates that Amanda and others in this current study fall into the 'high' creatives group since they share similar traits to those in Reiger's study. For example, as Reiger finds:

> The High Creatives seem to maintain a stronger sense of personal independence ... Career commitment was strikingly intense in both groups, but particularly among the High Creatives ... (and) Significant

differences in family and career patterns also were found, with Highs choosing to concentrate on career responsibilities only or to handle career and family roles simultaneously.

(p.98)

These results echo Helson (1999) who set out to find if there were patterns in women who became, as she calls it, 'future careerists' in the sense of remaining creative throughout their working lives. Like Reiger (1983), the qualities of independence and of prioritising their careers at least alongside their personal lives, if not above them, are evident in her findings. She asserts that '(w)omen with creative potential have a moratorium on identity, resisting commitment and remaining open to input that might modify who they are and how they construct the world' (p.98). All such characteristics are evident in the women interviewed for this study, and the next chapters pick up some of these threads in relation to hard work and determination, perceptions of themselves as creative, as well as choices made around one's personal life.

References

Arts Council. (2020) *Arts Council individual awards 2019: Report on gender statistics.* Available at: https://www.artscouncil.ie/Publications/Strategic-development/ Individual-Awards-2019-Report-on-Gender-Statistics/ (Accessed: 4 April 2022).

Arts Council. (2021) *Diversity and Arts Council awards: Report on gender, disability and ethnicity in individual awards in 2020.* Available at: https://www.artscouncil .ie/uploadedFiles/wwwartscouncilie/Content/About/Equality,_Human_Rights _and_Diversity/Diversity%20and%20Arts%20Council%20Awards_March %202021.pdf (Accessed: 4 April 2022).

Brooks, G.S. and Daniluk, J.C. (1998) 'Creative labors: The lives and careers of women artists', *The Career Development Quarterly*, 46(3), pp. 246–261. https:// doi.org/10.1002/j.2161-0045.1998.tb00699.x.

Cameron, D. (2018) *Feminism*. London: Profile Books.

Chadwick, W. (1990) *Women, art, and society*. London: Thames and Hudson.

Conor, B., Gill, R. and Taylor, S. (2015) 'Introduction: Gender and creative labour', in Conor, B., Gill, R. and Taylor, S. (eds.) *Gender and creative labour*. Chichester: Wiley-Blackwell, pp. 1–23.

Helson, R. (1999) 'A longitudinal study of creative personality in women', *Creativity Research Journal*, 12(2), pp. 89–101. https://doi.org/10.1207/ s15326934crj1202_2.

Holt, F. and Lapenta, F. (2010) 'Introduction: Autonomy and creative labour', *Journal for Cultural Research*, 14(3), pp. 223–229. https://doi.org/10.1080 /14797581003791453.

Jones, D. and Pringle, J.K. (2015) 'Unmanageable inequalities: Sexism in the film industry', in Conor, B., Gill, R. and Taylor, S. (eds.) *Gender and creative labour*. Chichester: Wiley-Blackwell, pp. 174–187.

Kaplan, J. (2020) *The genius of women: From overlooked to changing the world.* Dutton: Penguin Random House.

Koppman, S. (2016) 'Different like me: Why cultural omnivores get creative jobs', *Administrative Science Quarterly*, 61(2), pp. 291–331. https://doi.org/10.1177 /0001839215616840.

Korsmeyer, C. (2004) *Gender and aesthetics: An introduction.* New York: Routledge.

Lubart, T. and Guignard, J.H. (2004) 'The generality-specificity of creativity: A multivariate approach', in Sternberg, R.J., Grigorenko, E.L. and Singer, J.L. (eds.) *Creativity: From potential to realization.* Washington, DC: American Psychological Association, pp. 43–56.

Mattern, J.L., Child, J.T., Vanhorn, S.B. and Gronewold, K.L. (2013) 'Matching creativity perceptions and capabilities: Exploring the impact of feedback messages', *Journal of Advertising Education*, 17(1), pp. 13–25.

Milestone, K. (2015) 'Gender and the cultural industries', in Oakley, K. and O'Connor, J. (eds.) *The Routledge companion to the cultural industries.* London and New York: Routledge, pp. 501–511.

Nochlin, L. (1971) 'Why have there been no great women artists?' in Baker, E. and Hess, T.B. (eds.) *Art and sexual politics.* New York: Macmillan, pp. 194–205.

Petrusich, A. (2020) 'Tori Amos believes the muses can help: A conversation about music, politics, and what you learn about America from being on the road', *The New Yorker*, 26 April. Available at: https://www.newyorker.com/culture/the-new -yorker-interview/tori-amos-believes-the-muses-can-help (Accessed: 4 April 2022).

Reis, S.M. (2002) 'Toward a theory of creativity in diverse creative women', *Creativity Research Journal*, 14(3–4), pp. 305–316. https://doi.org/10.1207/ S15326934CRJ1434_2.

Rieger, M.P. (1983) 'Life patterns and coping strategies in high and low creative women', *Journal for the Education of the Gifted*, 6(2), pp. 98–110. https://doi .org/10.1177/016235328300600205.

Selby, E.C., Shaw, E.J. and Houtz, J.C. (2005) 'The creative personality', *Gifted Child Quarterly*, 49(4), pp. 300–314. https://doi.org/10.1177/001698620504900404.

Seligman, M.E. and Csikszentmihalyi, M. (2000) 'Positive psychology: An introduction', *American Psychologist*, 55(1), pp. 5–14.

Thomas, N.G. and Berk, L.E. (1981) 'Effects of school environments on the development of young children's creativity', *Child Development*, 52(4), pp. 1153–1162. https://doi.org/10.2307/1129501.

Wing-Fai, L., Gill, R. and Randle, K. (2015) 'Getting in, getting on, getting out? Women as career scramblers in the UK film and television industries', in Conor, B., Gill, R. and Taylor, S. (eds.) *Gender and creative labour.* Chichester: Wiley-Blackwell, pp. 174–187.

4 Creative work

Exploring resilience, work ethic, and motherhood

At the time that interviews were carried out, these women were established in their careers, some for many years, and others more recently. The ways in which they approached and managed their creative lives and work reveal some general patterns shared among them. For one, issues of time management and implementing certain work structures and practices – especially for those women with children – prove to be critical in enabling them to sustain a creative productivity. These creative women who were also mothers make very conscious choices and use various strategies which mean they can give themselves to both motherhood and their creative practices. Overall, these women exhibit strong levels of self-belief in their creative abilities and express a satisfaction at where they find themselves now in their creative lives. This self-belief is forthright and strong in some interviewees, while in others there is a quiet confidence that proved to not be easily shaken over the years. And they demonstrate, for the most part, that they are unconcerned with issues of sex and gender, especially those women who are a little older.

Sex and gender: how it has (and has not) played a role

The subject of sex and gender is one that underpins this entire study. However, this section expressly foregrounds this topic and teases out the consideration of whether and how these aspects have played a role in the approach and indeed the working lives of these creative women. In general, as mentioned above, there is little explicit interest or preoccupation with one's sex articulated by these interviewees. Instead, they tend to just get on with their creative work without overly thinking about gender and its effects. While there are some barriers and challenges perceived as a result of their sex, mostly the women do not dwell on such experiences or perceptions. Much of the literature on gender and creativity tells a different story, however, one that indicates that gender, sexism, and gender essentialist

DOI: 10.4324/9781003082750-4

ideas still impact on women's opportunities and how they and their work are perceived in the creative industries. As previously discussed at length, there is a long history of a gendered worldview which maintains that women's fate is one of inevitable creative mediocrity since women's place in the home necessarily meant they would never be able to elevate their thinking to the heights required of creative excellence. Within societies which conceived of women as creatively inferior to men, the art world replicated such views. As Chadwick (1990) points out, '(b)y the nineteenth century, the polarization of male and female creativity was complete' (p.26). By this point, women's creative work was consistently dismissed, diminished, and denigrated. She maintains (p.23) that a gendered lens and associated language of 'masculine' and 'feminine' styles and approaches to art figured in all conversations and evaluations of art. Consequently, one cannot talk of an 'objective' assessment or appraisal of women's work since it was automatically considered 'feminine' and therefore less valued or skilled than that of their male counterparts.

The aspect of external validation and how their work is understood and reviewed can have dire consequences from women. The general underrating of women's creative work impacts how they work, with Henry (2009) suggesting that '(w)hile men's creative outputs tend to result in increased professional stature and financial gain, women's creative efforts are often diversified over several initiatives and appear more modest' (p.151). It is not surprising that women's creative work may seem more piecemeal and stop-start given that women are not considered the equals of their male peers. This is to say that the lukewarm reception of their work, which many creative women have had to contend with over the course of decades – indeed, centuries – of art, literature, and creative practice arguably amount to 'confidence-destroying experiences' (Thomas and Berk, 1981), as discussed in the preceding chapter, and could result in less sustained and prolific creative careers. And although opinions have certainly changed and improved since Léon Legrange proclaimed in 1860 in the *Gazette des Beaux-Arts* 'let men busy themselves with all that has to do with great art. Let women occupy themselves with those types of art which they have always preferred, such as pastels, portraits, and miniatures' (cited in Chadwick, 1990, p.35), gendered attitudes, albeit more subtle, around women's suitability to creative work have endured.

Some would argue that women lack the kind of single-mindedness needed to be effective creators and creatives and that something in their nature impacts their ability to be creatively productive. Reis (2002) notes that '(a) nother reason why fewer creative women fulfill their potential to complete professional and creative endeavors seems to revolve around differential priorities' (p.311), ones that factor in their relationships and responsibilites to others in ways that men do not. But even if one accepts that men and women are different in ways that are significant, women have simultaneously been traditionally discouraged from exploring and centring what are specifically female experiences in their art and creative work if they want to be taken seriously. For instance, in the 1940s and 1950s, at a time when the creative world was opening up to women, female artists faced a dilemma:

> Many women artists, encouraged by their teachers not to link art practice with female experience in order to succeed, confronted the difficulty inherent in refusing socially assigned notions of difference while continually pointing to difference and questioning its influence and effects.
> (Chadwick, 1990, pp.302–303)

This indicates that female artists cannot win. They can never be considered simply 'artists' or 'creators' without the prefix of 'women', but at the same time, they must not be too 'female' in their approach or chosen subject matter. Interviewees for this study were asked such questions that invited them to reflect on differences between the sexes, specifically, whether they could identify discernible differences in the creative outputs of men and women. Their responses were highly interesting.

Jess Kavanagh put forward the view that there may be something identifiably female about the women working in the music industry. She says:

> There's a lot more powerful and fearless self-reflection and self-inspection in music that's written by women and I think there's less of that with men and I think that is because within the patriarchal structures there's not as much emphasis on men to do emotional work.

Yet, this is something she sees changing, with hopeful signs of men supporting other men to start to engage with their emotional selves and take responsibility for their actions and behaviours, particularly in intimate relationships. Nevertheless, as things stand, women are

> expected not only to nurture ourselves but to nurture others and generally speaking men tend not to do emotional work and so you tend to hear that in music and in the lyrical content of the music that is being written. It's about women coming into their power and what they've learnt from experiences and the perspective in a lot of men's music is the external happening to them where the accountability is lower.

Considering the question of what stories, topics, or themes Lisa Mulcahy feels drawn to in choosing to direct a script, she explains they tend to be well-written stories that reflect universal human experiences. While she does not think female directors have a discernible style or signature in their work, she laments the fact that the industry still remains heavily male in terms of director roles, even if the situation is improving. She points out the ludicrousness of this since 'it's not like men understand violence better than women do or ... (that) women understand love better than men do. There is no reason for that because it's all emotions and we all have the same emotions'. Similarly, on this question of whether women create recognisably 'female' works, Marina Carr says:

> The first impulse is you know you create out of who you are but then you have to allow for the imaginative journey, you know? Each artist is completely different, where that falls in with gender I wouldn't like to say ... it's not a helpful bandwidth for either men or women to be assigned that, I think that's part of the difficulty that we are trying to deal with now is being put in separate camps.

In other words, we are limited by gender and we should not be hung up on things like a distinctly female experience or view of the world since these things risk closing down creative avenues. Having said that and having rejected essentialist understandings of the sexes and the works they create, Marina notes that working and collaborating with women brings a different kind of experience and energy than when she works with men. Having worked with an increasing number of women in the past few years, as directors, lighting designers, and composers, these collaborations have a distinct 'quality' whereby, when women work together, it tends to be a relationship that is 'fruitful' and a little easier to navigate whereas, she seems to suggest, those working dynamics are trickier with men because of an 'unnatural fear of the empowerment of women'. Amanda Coogan also discusses the importance of working and collaborating with other women which, given the importance of the body to her practice, is no surprise. She says, 'I invite other women to perform with me because I think my work is so centred around the female body that in some ways that makes sense and then I do like to buck the statistics'. What these accounts from Marina and Amanda attest to is that, while not necessarily essentialising the 'female experience', there is a kind of shorthand that exists between women which makes working with one another both satisfying and productive. This idea of being productive is a loaded one for women. Descriptions of artists and creatives struggling with productivity are often described as 'barren' with '(b)arren ... one of those words that for the longest time ... has been associated with a woman's value, with being incapable of producing offspring. This concept contains an unjust finality in it' (Amos, 2020, p.243). While women may reject these connotations, sexist attitudes still prevail in the CCIs, albeit in a diminished state. And it's a reality that this cohort of women are either aware of or encountered during their careers.

Oonagh Kearney, for one, reflects on the topic of industry bias in Ireland and recalls applying for and receiving funding from Screen Ireland in 2010 for a short film, and noting that of the eight recipients, she was the only female filmmaker. 'I felt that was wrong', she says. She believes that on another occasion, she may have been subject to unconscious bias in having a script rejected for funding with a note from one of the readers commenting that the story was 'quite domestic', something Oonagh resented and pushed back on. While she sees positive change and genuine, concerted effort and investment in ensuring that women can succeed in the Irish film industry, she believes there is still some way to go until parity is reached. One of the stumbling blocks to achieving this goal is fatigue with the topic of women in creative work. Oonagh herself admits:

> Sometimes I feel like I'm sick of all the women stuff, like I just want to be a filmmaker you know but other days I'm like but being a woman is such an amazing thing and actually it's such an important part of my identity.

She talks generally about the cultural, industry, and organisational shifts that need to occur in the filmmaking process and notes that it would benefit both men and women if the issue of care and caring responsibilities was normalised in the industry and if women's careers were not disadvantaged if and when they need to take a step back. Una Healy similarly feels she faced discrimination on the basis of her sex on some occasions. Her years working in London were hectic, exciting, and successful. Although she was promoted in all the roles she was in and ended up managing a department, she was aware of a bias in favour of male colleagues because of the perception that even if they became fathers it wouldn't impact their working days in the ways it would for mothers. However, this is something she sees changing, in that there's now greater acceptance of the need for organisations to be flexible with their employees in terms of hours and where they can and might work. For Lelia Doolan, one of the most challenging experiences of her professional life has come in recent years in her involvement with Tracy Geraghy on the founding of the Pálás Cinema in Galway: 'the only place recently that I have felt that being a woman was a disadvantage to the work at hand was when I was building the cinema in Galway'. She had to contend with working with a team of all-male civil service employees and found the process difficult. She maintains that 'if we were two men who were running that project it would've been a different story'.

Jess discusses her experiences of sexism in the music industry and points out that there is a sense that the industry only has room for a certain number of women and instead of supporting, collaborating, and embracing other female singers and musicians, women perceive themselves in competition with each other. As she says, 'there is still such an issue of tokenism and there is still such an issue with "if I'm here another woman can't be here as well" you know', but she sees this as something that is diminishing with a growing camaraderie among Irish women singers, bands, and musicians. While a healthier and more supportive environment for women in the Irish music industry may be emerging, Jess's previous experiences of touring with men who are 'difficult' is still a cause of upset. She talks about the prototypically male touring musician as the

50-year-old who hasn't been home in like 20 years who has kind of emotionally distanced himself from his whole family and kind of blames women for it so is just kind of going on these horrendous Daily Mail fucking seasoned tirades every time he has a couple of pints and you have to just fucking sit there and take it.

Similar to the point made about feeling in competition with each other as women, Jess touches on the 'internalised sexism' that can manifest in women, and she talks about a suggestion she made to a friend years ago about setting up a support network for women musicians to talk about the challenges they face in the industry, only for that suggestion to be shot down by her friend as unfairly exclusionary of men. But tackling industry bias towards women is easier said than done since if you call out sexist behaviours, it can lead to very uncomfortable working environments and can result in women 'getting a reputation of being difficult'.

After working in TV production design and later, more briefly, in film, Annie West has latterly worked as a children's illustrator and a cartoonist. She talks about it being impossible to get a fair shot at publication because she was on the outside of a kind of boy's club. There's palpable frustration evident in her telling of the blood, sweat, and tears poured into creating cartoons for submission to the *Irish Times* and other newspapers which 'never got published'. This led her to wondering whether to just 'pack it in':

When I was trying to get work as a cartoonist, I was sending stuff into papers before the internet and it was soul-destroying because you would do a really, really beautiful visual, funny gag and put a huge amount of ... up all night, because you had to, because it was current. And send it into them real quick ... But it never got published ... And then you'd see something almost identical by Martin Turner and you'd go 'why do I bother trying to do this stuff?' you know and you'd sort of go, 'really, do I just pack it in?' and there'd been lots and lots of times where I just thought I'm so pissed off now that I, you know, I'm not getting anywhere, I can't get this together, it's not me or maybe it is and yet everybody else seems to find it dead easy.

In a more general discussion about the gendered and sexist environment that women and girls must navigate, Marina maintains that despite a breaking down of strict gender norms and accounting for the fact that most men are good, decent people 'trying to get by like most women', there still remains a very significant additional psychological burden on women about how they should 'be'. She says, 'I think women spend a lot of time just trying to "be", you know, without all this stuff being put onto them about who they are and what they mean'. She suggests that the girl child *knows* at some deep, fundamental level that the society she is growing up in considers her a little less valuable – or a lot less, depending on the culture –than her brothers, her male peers, and her male friends:

> I don't know do we think about it enough but it has to go in at some very, very cellular hardwiring level that we know in our heart and souls that we're not equal and what does that do to the girl child, do you know? Like, forget about us, we're adults, we're kind of made now for better or for worse and we're made in the patriarchal mould let's face it … [but] when you think of girl children and all the signals being picked up – as we would have picked up – that you are somehow, you're just a little bit less equal, you know, with all the best will in the world, the best father and mother in the world that message is still there.

This certainly resonates with the persistent patriarchal and binary world-view which operates hierarchically by assigning masculine–male traits and qualities a higher value than feminine–female ones. Marina is also critical of the fact that those who are revered and held up as templates and role models for both male and female writers, playwrights, and poets are always the 'Becketts', which is to say the male figures who make up the canon. The problem, as she sees it, is that 'we don't have the "power role models" as women you know … it's not that the work hasn't been written but it's been written and not rated, and just thrown aside'. Marina's critique of the culture's devaluing of women's work echoes arguments made by many, including Chadwick (1990), Korsmeyer (2004), and Henry (2009).

Women being overlooked for and even within creative roles in the CCI's is increasingly well-documented, as is the issue of discrimination, exploitation, and sex-based challenges for women in the creative sphere.

That narrative can be a difficult one to accept by those working in the industries, with Taylor and O'Brien (2017) noting that 'almost everyone believes that hard work, talent, and ambition are essential to getting ahead, while class, gender, ethnicity, and coming from a wealthy family are not' (p.17) but those most resistant to evidence that sex, among other markers, plays a role in success in the creative industries are men. However, as Jones and Pringle (2015) point out, feminists and advocates for women's advancement in the film industry have been at pains to highlight the fact that the data which shows how poorly women are faring across a range of roles in the industry cuts against the 'perception of gender equity' (p.7). In other words, while there may be reluctance on the part of many in the creative industries to do the requisite soul-searching as to why women are not succeeding at the rate they arguably should, in the meantime they and the organisations and firms they work in and for perpetuate a gender hierarchy with respect to creative versus other roles. Milestone (2015) attests to this pattern in her study of gender in the cultural industries which finds that those she interviewed espoused essentialist viewpoints about the supposed 'natural' aptitude of women and men to certain types of work. The upshot of these beliefs is that women end up occupying 'lower paid, low status jobs that are distanced from frontline creative production' (p.505). Nixon (2003) also found such attitudes within his study cohort of advertising practitioners who, despite perceptions to the contrary, reproduce rigid and indeed traditional gendered strata with high-status creative roles assigned largely to men, while women assumed more organisational, logistical, or relational client-facing roles.

More than a decade after Nixon's study, Hesmondhalgh and Baker (2015) identified the same issue whereby '(a)ssociations of various modes of masculinity with creativity ... serve to marginalise women from the more prestigious creative roles and even sectors in the cultural industries' (p.34). This results in, they argue, a kind of sex segregation in the CCIs. The consequence of this is that creative women continue to be disadvantaged by the persistence of the stereotype that they are better suited to the kind of work that facilitates men's creativity rather than taking on creative roles themselves. O'Brien (2014) documents similar disadvantages that impact on women in the Irish TV industry, with gendered assumptions about women being perceived by viewers as less authoritative than men. For instance, she quotes from one interviewee being told by a producer that a 'documentary would be taken more seriously with a male voice over' (p.7). The research of creativity scholars, like Baer and Kaufman (2008), offer a serious challenge to such essentialist views held by many in the creative industries and the wider society about women's lack of capacity for strong creative work relative to men. In their APT model of creativity, which attempts to map out the various components necessary for creative work, they note that – along with the specific range of skills and aptitudes that go along with each field and sub-field of creative work – there is the aspect of what they call 'initial requirements'. This refers to 'things that are necessary (but not sufficient) for any type of creative production — notably intelligence, motivation, and suitable environments' (p.77). It's in the category of environment that we see diverging experiences for men and women, with the authors noting that women's underachievement in being able to excel in creative fields can, in part, be explained by the 'lack of supporting environments ... the failure to nurture early talent ... (and) the control of entry into many fields and their resources by men' (p.77).

Women and girls have long recognised that fewer opportunities may come their way than their male counterparts. As such, there is an understanding that, in order to stand out, they must work far harder than their male peers. However, this drive to be outstanding and 'perfect' may not best serve talented women. In discussing the pattern of high-achieving teenage girls determined to do well across the board, as well as in the subjects they most love and excel at, Kaplan (2020) notes the drawbacks to this: 'Perfectionism is a great ingredient for mainstream success – but not so good for genius. Being too much of a stickler for conventional recognition tamps out any intellectual risk taking. Genius requires boldness and a bit of audacity' (p.233). In other words, if there's too much pressure and focus on being good at everything, and on being nice and liked, the conditions for enabling creative genius to flourish may be harder to put in place. Regardless, women understand that, until things change, they must outperform their male peers to even be considered a worthy insider in various fields. Annie discusses this issue by making reference to her belief that there's an awful lot more pressure on women these days: 'they have to be perfect' and 'have to never seem to be complaining about the thing. Feck that!' And if women do bring up workplace or work practice issues, they're considered 'hot heads' or 'hysterical women'.

Nevertheless, even for those creative women who are aware of the sexist double-standard, there's a determination to not be defined by their sex and its corresponding gendered expectations or to be beaten down by unfair gendered barriers. And, as previously mentioned, some of the interviewees articulated a lack of interest with issues connected to gender. For instance, on the question of whether women and men create art that is differentiated by their sex, Liz O'Kane says that it doesn't occur to her to view art through that lens and it doesn't 'interest' her to do so. She goes on to talk about her field of sculpture as male dominated as a result, she thinks, of the work being 'quite physical'. And while there are also other female sculptors, she enjoys the company and peer support from male colleagues. Lisa also seems to have dwelt rarely – if at all – on the question of sex/gender.

> I've never thought I couldn't do something because I was a woman. I never operated that way ... I don't recall my mother saying it but I have always figured that if I wanted something I could do it ... and okay I'm sure I ... probably have been knocked back in my career because I am a woman but of course it's something I can never prove and it's also something I have never dwelled on.

Annie articulates a similar position in that she's conscious of the challenges that gender poses, and suspects that some work likely did not come her way because of her sex but she stresses the need for women to be resilient in the face of rejection and disappointment; to just 'get over it'.

The instinct on the part of these women to not dwell on the obstacles or to become fixated on the challenges of gender and sexism tallies with research (Kaplan, 2020) that finds that women who stay focused and who don't get brow-beaten by real and perceived barriers are more likely to stick it out and succeed in their chosen fields. Discussing the fact that women may face significant barriers, Kaplan (2020) summarises conversations she had with Dr Frances Arnold, a recipient of the Nobel Prize in chemistry in 2018. Dr Arnold advises women to 'face the world in a powerful and positive way' (2020, p.254) and to not be overly focused on negatives. Dr Arnold 'thinks it's a detriment to young women now that "they are surrounded by this constant negative view that men are out to get them – and it's not true. Some men are – but you just avoid them"' (p.253–254). In other words, an over-emphasis on seeing oneself as a victim works against the kind of resilience and fearlessness required to succeed and excel. It is likely more helpful to creative women who wish to carve out a viable creative career for themselves to disregard and overcome gender and its attendant norms and expectations. This tendency is one that is strongly present in this study's cohort and is reflected in a recurrent theme of 'self-determination' that Brooks and Daniluk (1998) identify in interviews with creative women. Evident in this theme, they point out, is that creative women who make a creative life and living for themselves 'generally approached their futures with a strong sense of optimism' (p.253) and they find ways to ensure that they took control of their creative lives.

Hard work and tenacity: just getting on with it

Instead of focusing on barriers, these women demonstrate exceptionally strong work ethics. There is significant evidence of resilience and determination, and a recognition of the importance of being organised and able to multitask and manage time well. Such traits may be especially important with regard to work in the CCIs, an arena which is notable for its insecurity and uncertainty. In Ireland, as Oliveira (2018) points out, policy reports attest to the 'precarious work conditions of the artist and creative worker' (p.33) and he notes that sex-disaggregated data shows that women artists are earning, on average, less than half of the yearly income of their male colleagues. These wage gaps warrant careful consideration. However, our contemporary society's 'relentless celebrations of "creativity" (and) ... lack of attention to *work*' (Conor, Gill and Taylor, 2015, p.2; emphasis in original) has meant that 'a powerful stereotype has taken root and flourished. This sees the typical "creative" as driven by passion to Do What You Love (DWYL), prepared to work for long hours for little or even no pay, and requiring minimal support' (ibid.). Taylor (2015) echoes this in calling out the harmful cultural narrative of self-sacrifice in the CCIs. Such caricatures of the creative person negate the urgency of the need to address issues of exploitation, harassment, and inequality. As noted elsewhere, the women in this study, in almost all cases, work for themselves. While this means they are less at risk of enduring the kind of harassment and discrimination from colleagues and bosses that women in more structured creative environments might be vulnerable to, they also don't benefit from the structure and 'more stable patterns of employment' (Wing-Fai, Gill and Randle, 2015, p.50) that are typical of established, bigger organisations. In other words, there are challenges alongside opportunities for women in carrying out their creative work in unstructured, freelance, and project-based forms.

O'Brien (2014) identifies the drawback of a long-working-hours culture that has become typical in much of the creative and media sector, with '(w)orkers ... expected to show unstinting commitment while the boundaries of the working day are expanded and complete availability for work becomes the norm' (p.2). Operating outside of these structures provides women with more flexibility and autonomy to determine their working lives. However, Taylor (2015) interrogates the phenomenon of creative women working for themselves, typically from their homes, and asks us to consider if this may represent a kind of 'new mystique'. Taylor's argument is a play on Betty Friedan's second-wave feminist text, *The Feminine Mystique*, where the 'new mystique' in Taylor's iteration – as opposed to Friedan's discussion of the mystique and appeal of the housewife role – is the seeming allure for many workers to work, for themselves, in creative fields. However, the reality (for both male and female workers) is often one of self-sacrifice and little meaningful payment. This is where the concept is analogous to the housewife. Annie picks up on this as a more recent change and notes that there is now an apparent ruthlessness in creative fields, which she finds 'scary'. There's a huge expectation to do work for free in exchange for 'exposure'. She says:

> This is the trouble now is that you have people who have no choice but to work for nothing to get this so-called 'exposure' and it enrages me so much because not only are they doing themselves a disservice but also it's undercutting everybody who is trying to make a living out of it.

In exploring the reasons why people are attracted to the prospect of freelancing or self-employment, Taylor (2015) suggests that this is in part because workers now have a different relationship to employers and organisations. There is no longer the same degree of loyalty to one's company as there used to be in the past and indeed '(w)orkers are less deferential and expect more autonomy' (p.176). Consequently, for those who are not keen to submit to an organisational work structure and who are 'eager to do interesting and satisfying work which uses their skills, and (are) willing to risk some earning disadvantage, might see working for themselves as a desirable alternative' (ibid.). In particular, women might be more drawn to work for themselves than men because of perceived flexibility which might better allow them to manage their lives in ways where they can balance and juggle work and family commitments.

For this reason, those women who find themselves working for themselves in some creative capacity have typically blurred the lines between work and home and will often work from home. While this has its advantages for women, the downside is that they tend to then lack their own 'workshop' space typically associated with creatives, and where creative work is arguably best achieved. Such spaces that are separate from the home also offer people a break and a respite from the strains and demands of caring for families and children. Time away from the home also sends a positive message that time that women take for themselves – something men, and especially male creatives, arguably rarely have to justify – is valued and valuable and is not, as it is often framed, a reflection of selfishness (Taylor, 2015, p.183). For women engaging in creative work at home, with children, they miss out on this and thereby risk replicating, to some degree, the 'trap' identified by Friedan, wherein she was critical of a society where women were largely confined to their homes and were not to be found out in the world. The findings of this study show that the women in this cohort who work from home make it productive to do so by establishing strict work routines and clearly demarcating their home lives from their working lives, while others rely on and treasure their studio spaces, away from home, which enables their work to get done.

The need to prioritise time for oneself to allow creativity to flourish is referenced by Lisa. She maintains that

> Creativity means headspace ... you need the opportunity just to sit and stare and ... when you're working and then you got three children and a husband and a dog and a cat and two guinea pigs and a house in the middle of nowhere and that's where you live, you don't have that space to think.

It's easier to carve out that headspace and to cultivate those conditions of focusing on the work when she's away from her family and can devote her entire attention to whatever project she's working. She recognises the difficulty of being pulled in different directions. For example, at times when she might be trying to write from home with her children there, she notes that 'it's impossible to get a clear train of thought'. She talks also about a kind of streamlining of her life so that she doesn't feel spread too thinly. This means that her energies largely only go into family and work, and that's it. For Amanda Coogan, she treasures her time in her studio space. She also references the same pull on her attention that Lisa talks about and conceives of herself as fairly single-minded when she needs to be and of being able to 'drop things' that do not serve her work. In other words, she can and does prioritises different 'duties' at different times. On the aspect of time, she notes that short windows of time are not sustainable or conducive to creative work. At some points, longer tranches need to be carved out or cleaved back to allow creative thoughts and actions to percolate or germinate. This is something she calls the '"picking your nose" days in the studio'. These are days that are

> kind of unfocused, you're not really sure because you need to let that kind of flow over you, you can't be always 'on' in a short-term way, you know? ... [women] allow themselves less time for that certainly ... you have to give yourself permission to do that.

It is clear, then, that to earn a living through one's creative labour, one must be exceedingly driven and motivated. These qualities may be generally more evident in the kinds of people drawn to creative work. Indeed, Poutanen and Kovalainen (2017) suggest that a prerequisite for involvement in creative labour is a 'deep commitment to the actual work' (p.162), and they argue that for such people, their sense of self and their personal and 'work identity' are bound up in their creativity. Meanwhile, Lubart and Guignard (2004) suggest that '(c)reativity-relevant personality attributes include perseverance, willingness to take risks, willingness to tolerate ambiguity, openness to new experiences, and individuality' (p.46). Brooks and Daniluk (1998) found similar traits in evidence in mapping out patterns in the lives and careers of creative women. The women in their study perceived themselves as outliers and of having a 'sense of being a pioneer' (p.254) in the way that they didn't tread expected and traditional paths for women. They note that 'the sense of being a pioneer more particularly involved risk-taking behavior and the seeking-out of new experiences in both the personal and the professional realms' (ibid.), and that '(n)ot only did they demonstrate a high degree of tolerance for the ambiguous and unknown elements in life's journey, they also expressed through word and action the desire to explore the unfamiliar and unconventional aspects of life' (ibid.). All these traits feature heavily in the creative women interviewed for this study, especially those aspects associated with openness to new experiences, taking risks, and being comfortable with not knowing what was around the corner. For instance, on moving back to Dublin, Una set up her own practice with a business partner, and that company did very well over the next seven years. Revealingly, Una says:

> Like, if somebody had said to me in school when I was say 14, you'll end up running two businesses I'd go 'no', I'd be the last person on Earth that I'd know who would do that so never say never, like again it's like I just thought that's, somebody has to be real pushy and out there and whatever and actually in my business if you're good at want you do and you're easy to work with and you get results, that's it, that's the winning formula so yeah so that's been my career path.

There is evidence of much innovativeness and tenacity in Una's accepting a graphic design job at the Open Training College when she was pregnant, and only then sorting out the computer and software needed that would enable her to work from home. This indicates how determined she was to make things work for her and she set about creating the conditions around her that would allow her to raise her children and also maintain a career and strong links with the industry. She also demonstrates a determination to stay on top of the latest innovations in graphic design and says, 'I like learning. I think if you stop learning it becomes boring, so I think you have to keep learning and there's always new stuff'. Carole Pollard was similarly adamant about maintaining links to the architecture profession and industry even when she was not a practising architect. For her, this meant a pivot to teaching and writing about architecture. Amanda also made a pivot after having her son. She shares a very honest admission of a 'terror of a lack of time and energy' as a consequence of becoming of mother, so she very purposely decided to commit to a practice-based PhD while her son was small so that she had to make work. This speaks to the sheer commitment and need for work of a creative nature.

Commitment also represents both Liz and Annie's approaches to their work. Liz recognises her strengths in her ability to multitask and to be organised and that these aspects are crucial to her creative productivity, which she credits to her previous career in business and translating: 'galleries always say that I'm their most organised artist'. For Annie, she relies on a very 'strict' work routine which means that she prioritises progressing her work during regular business hours and simultaneously resents the expectation to respond to work-related calls and emails outside the usual working day. Interestingly, she has built the film *All the President's Men* into her work strategy, whereby she leaves the film playing in the background while she's working and, once it starts, she takes this as her cue to start work and not break until the film is over.

In terms of creative practice and the conditions for productivity, contrary to some myths that suggest a need for single-mindedness and absolute focus on just 'the work', Marina's view of this is that,

> to be single-minded is a huge disadvantage, it's going to limit to your practice, whatever your craft is. I think to be multi various and to have that capacity, to have empathy will ... make you better at it, give you a greater understanding. I just don't buy that at all, and I think, you know, this kind of ruthless, single-minded 'sacrifice everything' you know for the art, that is very much a male paradigm.

Marina brilliantly and passionately punctures the myth of the genius/artist whose work pours out of him. This myth elides the reality of the hard work and the 'plodding', as she puts it, that goes into creative work.

The lives, choices, and creative work trajectories of this study's cohort echo arguments put forward by Reis (2002). In a reference to Van Tassel-Baska's 1995 study on Charlotte Brontë and Virginia Woolf, Reis explains that Tassel-Baska suggested three common 'themes' in the lives of the writers that contributed to their succes, namely, *adversity,* a determination to not let challenges and barriers stand in their way; *autodidactism,* a willingness to seek out knowledge and training on their own, without traditional structures that typically support the passing on of requisite skills; and *emotional support*, the importance of encouragement and mentorship (p.309). This tracks with the findings of this study concerning the importance of tenacity and support as two of the most important factors to continuing and excelling in creative work.

Motherhood: its impacts and its absence

Six of the ten women are mothers, and all show their commitment to their creative careers and lives in the strategies they adopt to ensure they can maintain their careers while being very involved mothers. In other words, those with children make very conscious choices that mean they can manage being mothers while still maintaining a link with their creativity. This speaks to the huge commitment and need for work of this nature that they don't take up alternative types of easier or more manageable work.

Motherhood and creativity have a contentious relationship. The 2021 film *The Lost Daughter*, directed by Maggie Gyllenhaal brilliantly depicts the maternal role and the tensions that exist between the love an academic has for her children and her responsibility and obligation to them versus her drive for freedom, personal and creative self-fulfilment, and ambition. Whatever of the challenges that face women involved in creative practice who become mothers, there is a general perception held in society that creativity and motherhood are not naturally linked. Karl Scheffler in his 1908 *Die Fraue und die Kunst* 'emphasized woman's inability to participate in the production of culture because of her ties to nature and her lack of spiritual insight' (Chadwick, 1990, p.270), thereby maintaining that the mother role is the antithesis to artistic practice. Rather than try to deny that motherhood has no bearing on creativity for women, Reis (2002) notes that women's creative work is simply different from men's, which seems to suggest that we can speak of a 'male creativity' and 'female creativity', a potentially essentialist viewpoint. She argues that '(s)ome female artists ... believe that the creative growth they experience from both child-birth and parenting can actually contribute to creative growth in their art' (p.309). The fact that men are so keen to claim the realm of creativity for themselves is a reflection of their envy of women's capacity to give birth (see work by US radical feminist and theologian Mary Daly on women as the creative, life-giving sex, with men as the jealous, destructive sex). Mothers, as Ruddick (1980) arued in her seminal text *Maternal Thinking*, are often simultaneously powerful and powerless in our societies. Their power resides in their role in reproducing the human race, but patriarchy operates in such ways as to deny her power in every other domain, not least culturally and creatively.

As discussed previously, the topic of women and creativity, in addition to the subject of male and female approaches to art and creativity, was raised with interviewees, with mixed opinions expressed about whether one can really say there are discernible differences between the sexes. In relation to these conversations, reference to single-mindedness as a prerequisite for creative productivity was discussed. Here again, there are diverging opinions among the women, with Amanda more firmly of the view that this is a critical trait to creative practice, while Marina rejects the proposition that having other pulls on one's attention and emotions negates good and sustained creative work. Kogan (1974) writes:

> It is a virtual truism to state that genuine creative accomplishment requires a single-minded dedication to particular goals and tasks. To the degree that an individual is distracted from such pursuits by the social context, the effect is bound to be lessened creativity.
>
> (p.12)

He suggests that women risk being at a disadvantage relative to men since they 'are more susceptible to ... distraction than are men' (ibid.). And, if this is the case, he calls on research to ascertain if women are naturally less inclined towards the kind of single-minded, unwavering attention that creative work demands or if women's environments and the social demands and expectations made of them play a role. Reis (2002), almost three decades later, also references this perception:

> Perhaps the most controversial issue related to women and the creative process is the claim that there may be a potential mismatch between the single-minded devotion necessary for creative accomplishment and the desire to balance family and career that appears so frequently in research about creative women.
>
> (p.309)

She points out that such a widely held misconception misses the point that, in multitasking and in occupying various roles – for example, as wife, mother, creative, entrepreneur, and so forth – women can, and do, switch between one role and another, and when occupying the creative role, they demonstrate the ability to be 'single-mindedly' focused on the task at hand. Reis references Richards (1996) when she points out that 'women have the potential to display single-minded devotion to their work, but they may also choose to diversify their creative efforts' (ibid.). In other words, they adopt strategies that enable them to fulful and excel in both the mothering and creative role. One has to wonder whether as many men, relative to women, would succeed if they were spread so thinly. In any case, this idea of women who are mothers being unsuited to creative work persists. Wing-Fai, Gill, and Randle (2015) identify a concerning presumption on the part of some of their study cohort who express the viewpoint that 'having children in some way "taints" or absorbs a woman's creative energy or will to succeed' (p.61). The authors point out that the same is not said of a new father's creative 'hunger'.

But is there evidence that creative mothers work less productively or in different ways? And is there simply less hunger? On the latter point, the conversations with the women in this study who are mothers do not bear this out. Amanda explains that she was 'very, very worried about motherhood' and the 'splitting' that might result from trying to be mother, artist, and sign-language-interpreter (SLI) all at once. She recognised that she wouldn't be able to sustain herself, creatively speaking, if she attempted to juggle all three roles, so she consciously made the decision to let the SLI take a back seat. She credits the early years of motherhood with making her super-efficient with her time during which she would very purposely earmark some time to do her own practice. Annie's hunger for creative work manifests in her decision to work differently. She turned to illustration when she was expecting her first child, 'because it was all I was able to do now that I was looking after a little baby'.

Three of the women in the study who are not mothers referenced ideas and attitudes connected to creative hunger, single-mindedness, freedom, and the notion of divided attentions. Lelia, who grew up at a time when women's options were more limited than they are now, reflects on the question of whether she felt she had to make certain life choices in order to continue and sustain the career she has carved out for herself over the years. She responds:

> I have to say I have been utterly and completely lucky in that I have never had a long enough relationship with anybody of any sex to stop me from doing anything I wanted to do so I have always been independent and free, I think freedom is one of the absolute epitomes of creativity, I think if you're not free you can't really be able to be creative and I have always had the good fortune to be free.

She goes on to define freedom as 'freedom from obedience to anything except one's own sense of rightness of the integrity of the thing that has to be done, that's what I would say'. And on the fact that she has, more or less, always lived alone, she believes this has meant she hasn't 'had to trim my sails in the sense to anything other than what I felt I needed to do because … [the] harrowing daily grind that some women … have to undergo, I didn't have to'.

Speaking on the topic of motherhood and what it means for life as a creative person, Jess understands herself to be someone who doesn't have a desire to be a mother. However, on this subject, she recounts a conversation with male friends on tour who were adamant that she should experience parenthood and insisted that 'it's such a wonderful thing being a parent'. She, astutely, responds by pointing out 'Your ability to be here is based on the fact that your partner had your child' and is at home. Jess notes that 'it's harder to take risks' if you have a child, particularly from a financial point of view. In other words, if you're responsible for other people, it's less likely that you can simply pick up and go on the road for months on end, something that 'session musicians' are often expected to do. Liz likewise touches on the importance of freedom to her creative life and work. She highly values the freedom afforded by the work she does in being able to travel and take up teaching posts in other cities and countries or simply 'pack up' her studio and create work elsewhere; such a life would not be as readily available to more conventional careers. A key aspect of her creative productivity is, she thinks, the more time she has at her disposal to work than colleagues and peers who have children:

> I'm lucky in that regard so that's a real luxury. I mean, of course it would be lovely to have kids but on the other side I have more time to devote to my sculpture and my career and I'm pretty good at multi-tasking all areas of my life so I think it would be a very different question and you would get very different answers from anybody who has children and the responsibilities and the worries and the concerns that happen with being a carer.

She goes on to explain how important friends and socialising are to her and describes herself as 'quite a free spirit' and as really enjoying that independence. 'I don't know', she says, 'how I would be if I was more tied down or had to stay in Dublin or had more responsibilities, I suppose my life would be very different'.

What is clear in these accounts of motherhood and caring, both by the mothers in the study and those who are not, is that the aspects of motivation and 'hunger' are conceived somewhat differently by both groups. For those who don't have children, they articulate an anxiety that creative avenues and a freedom to prioritise one's work would close down if they were mothers. While those who are mothers similarly exhibit this concern, the fact that they find ways to maintain that appetite for creative work is testament to women's ability to shape the conditions of their lives and the demands on their time to enable them to remain involved in creative work. Nevertheless, the strategies employed by creative women who are mothers can manifest in what Brooks and Daniluk (1998) identify as 'being torn between the needs of self and others' (p.252). Regardless, women with children address this pressure in whatever ways they find best work for them. However, despite their best efforts, it is not always possible to maintain one's career in the CCIs in the face of considerable social, environment, and industry challenges that make things difficult for mothers in creative fields.

In a study focusing largely on social class as a determinant of getting into and progressing with the creative industries in the UK, Brook, O'Brien, and Taylor (2018) make the case that 'cultural and creative industries, for the population born in the 1950s and after, have always been socially exclusive' (p.32). The report details that, of particular concern, is the trend for mothers to drop out of work in the creative industries. Women in the media industries, a report commissioned by the European Parliament (McCracken et al., 2018) notes, face significant sex discrimination in the form of abuse and harassment, issues with career advancement, and a gender pay gap. It is also noted that organisations in the industries do not cater for women who become mothers, resulting in a considerable handicap for these women. Jones and Pringle (2015) find the same issues in the film industry in New Zealand, with women opting out of the industry at a time when they want to start a family as a result of the lack of supports with respect to maternity leave and childcare. The upshot of these trends, as Conor, Gill, and Taylor (2015) point out, is that the majority of women working in the CCIs are typically relatively young and 'less likely than their male counterparts to have children' (p.7). Wing-Fai, Gill, and Randle (2015) also identify this pattern of more fathers than mothers working in creative media.

The extent to which fatherhood doesn't impact on men's career creatives is tracked in Milestone's (2015) study, wherein she notes that male colleagues have little idea about each other's home lives and whether or not they have children. This speaks to the taken-for-granted nature of the labour at home undertaken by the wives and partners of these men. Arguably it's not possible for women to operate home and work as such separate spheres since there's a greater degree of overlap between these areas of women's lives given that women take on more of the responsibility for child-caring and rearing than their male partners. Such is this reality that organisations in the creative industries may feel justified in opting to hire men over women who may have children at some point during their employment (Wing-Fai, Gill, and Randle, 2015). Outside the more structured setting of companies and organisations, women who work for themselves and who are also mothers 'experience problems balancing business and family commitments' (Henry, 2009, p.15). As noted, this study's cohort have opted to operate outside established work structures and have created careers working, largely, for themselves in project-based or freelance ways. Reis (2002) suggests that women involved in creative work will opt to work in ways that enable them to best manage demands of family life with their careers. As much as the choice to be very involved mothers is a rewarding one for many creative women, the result of this balancing of roles is often in being less prolific than their male colleagues. This can impact on how their body of work is assessed and whether they are deemed creatively successful or not. Not surprisingly, research has found that creative women commonly report feelings of guilt in terms of spending time away from children and family in order to work, as well as having to deal with 'considerable stress related to role conflict and overload, which may reduce creative urges ... Both external and internal barriers affect creativity in women' (Reis, 2002, p.309–310). Many men, however, are free of this mental load, the so-called 'double shift', as well as the emotional labour that women continue to take on. The 'great conflict' that Reis references is likely part biological, part social pressure – for example, manifesting as guilt for any time spent away from children – and part environment, for instance, the challenge of how to navigate relationships with partner or spouse and the issue of child-care and housework.

There is much of the above that tracks with the experiences of the creative women interviewed for this study. Carole shares a very telling experience of early motherhood. When she was expecting her first child, she remembers there being much excitement and support from her colleagues. She was working in a small architecture firm at the time and had a strong personal relationship with her employers. During the months of her pregnancy they had assured her that they were fully supportive of her, but the reality when she had her daughter was one in which she felt she was not given the consideration or flexibility needed to manage the two roles. She ultimately left that organisation, setting up her own practice so she could manage the two. This experience echoes the research showing that many women in the creative industries find themselves struggling to cope with work pressures and structures that are inflexible to the needs of mothers. Nevertheless, Carole suggests that not agonising over the choice to have her first child was just as well, since it meant she simply had to make something work for her; although she expresses some regret and resentment that her career never reached the heights she had thought it would. She suggests that she feels that, on balance, her career was sacrificed in order to be able to be a fully present mother to her children and that if she had tried it any other way, she would have had a 'breakdown'. Even though her career was scaled back, she found motherhood offered tonnes of opportunities to be playful and creative; this, she acknowledges, was enabled by the financial security provided by her husband.

Una similarly scaled back on work commitments when expecting her first child. This involved selling her shares in the business she founded and leaving that organisation behind. This decision took her, somewhat, by surprise:

> I always thought I'd be a career woman so I was pregnant and I thought 'oh my God I don't want anyone else minding this baby', so I sold

my shares in the business and that sort of made it okay for myself and my husband, the mortgage went so we didn't have that pressure on us and then what happened after that was like I had three kids but during that time people used to ring me and go 'hey, you used to do graphic design could you do this job for us?' And the whole thing just literally grew from there so as the kids got bigger and I'd more free time, I was doing more work until it was what it is now today, so we just grew very organically.

In evidence here is, as Reis (2002) refers to it, the choice to work in ways that 'facilitate' both motherhood and creative work. For Una, the dilemma is when the two roles come into conflict. She maintains that it's very hard to be creatively productive when children are small and it would have been totally unfeasible in the working environments she was in in London, with long hours and expectations that such caring responsibilities wouldn't impinge on work.

Of great importance to Lisa is the aspect of having a partner who is very hands-on with regards to running a household with her. In other words, the intensely creative work of filmmaking means that she requires a solid system of support, and she talks about the importance of having an equal partnership with her husband, with whom she splits the caring responsibilities. This enables her to spend long periods on location shooting, filming, and directing. She acknowledges that 'if I was a single mother, I just simply couldn't do it, if I was a single father, I just simply couldn't do it you know'. Motherhood, and the responsibilities that come with that, certainly make it more 'difficult' for women to endure in their respective creative fields. For Marina, she suspects that having her children a bit later when she was already fairly established with a significant body of work helped. And while she acknowledges the challenges of having small kids and trying to maintain the kind of career that involves hard work and self-motivation, she points to the positive changes in society in that women are benefitting from more involved partners and husbands:

It's more doable I think now, and I don't think it's necessarily a bad thing to try and, you know, to want it all ... I wanted the whole circus, I wanted ... to be married, I wanted children and I wanted to continue to write and managed to do it, maybe not as much as I would have done had I been, had I not married and had children but you know that's not the choice I made, the choice I made was I wanted that, I wanted everything and ... my experience of that is that, you know, my children or my husband have never held me back.

Again, in this account and assessment of motherhood and its effect on creative work, the challenges are apparent, but there is similarly satisfaction and joy from 'having it all'. Marina's reference to the situation having improved in terms of women now benefitting from more involved husbands, partners, and fathers is an important one. Oonagh, although not a mother herself, identifies a shift in filmmaking circles, with a greater and growing emphasis on setting up the conditions within the industry and the filmmaking process to enable both male and female film workers to take leave when they need to. She mentions the Raising Films initiative set up in the UK, which aims to practically tackle the issue of parenting and carer responsibilities for those crew working on film:

> I know a number of practitioners – writer, directors, producers – who are about ten years younger than me and I think they are in their early 30s and they're kind of having this conversation now and I think it's healthy that they've had that and they feel empowered to sort of say what they want and sort of to pursue it.

This anecdote points to tentative evidence of a change of mindset among men and women working in the film industry and offers a reminder that, if men join with their female colleagues in normalising the balancing of parenthood with creative work, both sexes would benefit.

References

Amos, T. (2020) *Resistance: A songwriter's story of hope, change, and courage.* New York: Atria Books: Sword and Stone Publishing Inc.

Baer, J. and Kaufman, J.C. (2008) 'Gender differences in creativity', *Journal of Creative Behavior*, 42(2), pp. 75–105. https://doi.org/10.1002/j.2162-6057.2008 .tb01289.x.

Brook, O., O'Brien, D. and Taylor, M. (2018) 'There was no golden age: Social mobility into cultural and creative occupations', *SocArXiv*, March 27. https://doi .org/10.31235/osf.io/7njy3.

Brooks, G.S. and Daniluk, J.C. (1998) 'Creative labors: The lives and careers of women artists', *The Career Development Quarterly*, 46(3), pp. 246–261. https:// doi.org/10.1002/j.2161-0045.1998.tb00699.x.

Chadwick, W. (1990) *Women, art, and society.* London: Thames and Hudson.

Conor, B., Gill, R. and Taylor, S. (2015) 'Introduction: Gender and creative labour', in Conor, B., Gill, R. and Taylor, S. (eds.) *Gender and creative labour.* Chichester: Wiley-Blackwell, pp. 1–23.

Henry, C. (2009) 'Women and the creative industries: Exploring the popular appeal', *Creative Industries Journal*, 2(2), pp. 143–160. https://doi.org/10.1386/cij.2.2 .143/1.

Hesmondhalgh, D. and Baker, S. (2015) 'Sex, gender and work segregation in the cultural industries', in Conor, B., Gill, R. and Taylor, S. (eds.) *Gender and creative labour*. Chichester: Wiley-Blackwell, pp. 23–36.

Jones, D. and Pringle, J.K. (2015) 'Unmanageable inequalities: Sexism in the film industry', in Conor, B., Gill, R. and Taylor, S. (eds.) *Gender and creative labour*. Chichester: Wiley-Blackwell, pp. 174–187.

Kaplan, J. (2020) *The genius of women: From overlooked to changing the world*. Dutton: Penguin Random House.

Kogan, N. (1974) 'Creativity and sex differences', *Journal of Creative Behavior*, 8(1), pp. 1–14.

Korsmeyer, C. (2004) *Gender and aesthetics: An introduction*. New York: Routledge.

Lubart, T. and Guignard, J.H. (2004) 'The generality-specificity of creativity: A multivariate approach', in Sternberg, R.J., Grigorenko, E.L. and Singer, J.L. (eds.) *Creativity: From potential to realization*. Washington, DC: American Psychological Association, pp. 43–56.

McCracken, K., FitzSimons, A., Priest, S., Girstmair, S. and Murphy, B. (2018) *Gender equality in the Media Sector*. Brussels: European Parliament. Available at: https://www.europarl.europa.eu/RegData/etudes/STUD/2018/596839/IPOL _STU(2018)596839_EN.pdf (Accessed: 4 April 2022).

Milestone, K. (2015) 'Gender and the cultural industries', in Oakley, K. and O'Connor, J. (eds.) *The Routledge companion to the cultural industries*. London and New York: Routledge, pp. 501–511.

Nixon, S. (2003) *Advertising cultures: Gender, commerce, creativity*. London and Thousand Oaks, CA: SAGE.

O'Brien, A. (2014) '"Men *own* television": Why women leave media work', *Media, Culture & Society* 36(8), pp. 1–12. https://doi.org/10.1177/01634437145 44868.

Oliveira, E. (2018) *An analysis of the cultural and creative industries in Ireland: Implications for policy-making*. PG diploma thesis. DIT School of Marketing. Available at: https://www.researchgate.net/publication/327655739 (Accessed: 4 April 2022).

Poutanen, S. and Kovalainen, A. (2017) *Gender and innovation in the new economy: Women, identity and creative work*. New York: Palgrave Macmillan.

Reis, S.M. (2002) 'Toward a theory of creativity in diverse creative women', *Creativity Research Journal*, 14(3–4), pp. 305–316. https://doi.org/10.1207/ S15326934CRJ1434_2.

Richards, R. (1996) 'Beyond Piaget: Accepting divergent, chaotic, and creative thought', in Runco, M. (ed.) *Creativity from childhood through adulthood: The developmental issues. New directions for child development*. San Francisco: Jossey-Bass, pp. 67–86.

Ruddick, S. (1980) 'Maternal thinking', *Feminist Studies*, 6(2), pp. 342–367. https:// doi.org/10.2307/3177749.

Taylor, M. and O'Brien, D. (2017) 'Culture is a meritocracy: Why creative workers' attitudes may reinforce social inequality', *Sociological Research Online*, pp. 1–21. https://doi.org/10.1177/1360780417726732.

Taylor, S. (2015) 'A new mystique? Working for yourself in the neoliberal economy', in Conor, B., Gill, R. and Taylor, S. (eds.) *Gender and creative labour*. Chichester: Wiley-Blackwell, pp. 174–187.

Thomas, N.G. and Berk, L.E. (1981) 'Effects of school environments on the development of young children's creativity', *Child Development*, 52(4), pp. 1153–1162. https://doi.org/10.2307/1129501.

Wing-Fai, L., Gill, R. and Randle, K. (2015) 'Getting in, getting on, getting out? Women as career scramblers in the UK film and television industries', in Conor, B., Gill, R. and Taylor, S. (eds.) *Gender and creative labour*. Chichester: Wiley-Blackwell, pp. 174–187.

5 Creative identities

Integrating creativity into sense of self and life satisfaction

As a general pattern among interviewees, the place of creativity in their lives is a very crucial one in contributing to their sense of self, and it provides an outlet for self-expression in ways that provide joy as well as feelings of contentment, fulfilment, and gratification. A development of an established creative identity plays a critical role in enabling them to persist and thrive in creative work; no mean feat given the challenges and insecurity inherent in such work (as discussed in the previous chapter). Their views on the label of 'artist' and 'creative' vary along generational lines, with Oonagh Kearney and Jess Kavanagh as the youngest women in the cohort expressing an ease with self-describing themselves in these terms in a way that some of the women older than them are not.

Creativity: brings inner strength, joy, and fulfilment

Evident in the interviews were themes associated with the women's identity, and a sense of deep fulfilment and joy extracted from the various creative fields in which they're involved. They all showed themselves to be curious, open-minded, warm, and joyful. Abuhamdeh and Csikszentmihalyi (2004), in exploring the characters of creative people and the question of whether there really is a singular artistic personality, draw on previous studies which find that creatives tend to be 'emotional … sensitive, independent, impulsive, and socially aloof … introverted … and nonconforming' (p.32). All of these traits are present in this study's cohort, with the exception of social aloofness. Instead, the women interviewed were all warm and engaging. They talked about the importance of creativity in their lives, with some noting that creativity can be defined in more broader terms than they might previously have imagined. On the topic of the diversification of creativity, Reis (2002) has commented that across the life span of creative women their 'creativity is diverted to multiple areas in their lives, including relationships, work related to family and home, personal interests, aesthetic

DOI: 10.4324/9781003082750-5

sensitivities, and appearances' (p.312). This expanded notion of creativity is important in terms of recognising the many ways that creative women find to give expression to their creativity. This is especially found in the conversations with Carole Pollard, Jess Kavanagh, and Una Healy and in how they talked about the myriad creative tasks they involve themselves with. In Jess's case, she sees herself

> more as a creative than just a musician ... I love drawing now and I love yoga and I love writing and I'm writing for the *Irish Times*, and I get to write professionally and I write poetry and I perform poetry and I perform spoken word and I also now sing and I also play piano.

Diversifying her creative interests and outputs has resulted in a shift in her identity and led to a healthier sense of herself as a more all-round creative person rather than having her identity tied up in one thing: being a singer. That narrower self-conceptualisation had become a burden in the sense that if she was faced with some weaknesses as a singer, it was difficult for her to process and accept. Given that she has constructed a new identity based on being 'creative' and being part poet/writer/artist and so on, those insecurities are lessened, leaving her freer to be expressive without fear of failing to live up to very high standards. Understanding creativity in a more wide-ranging sense puts the focus on process rather than output or outcome – or, to put it another way, it focuses on the journey rather than the destination. However, in reference to a 1996 paper by herself, Reis says that while some women place a lot of value in the wide range of creative tasks they get involved in, others end up feeling frustrated and resentful that they could not – often for the reason of being pulled in too many directions – channel those creative energies towards more directed, professional activities as their male peers had done. There is some evidence of this frustration evident in the findings of this study, especially from Carole and Annie West, but both express greater levels of fulfilment in more recent years and greater satisfaction with where they're at now. In Carole's case, she notes that

> It's only really since I went back to teach second year architecture in 2017 that I really have had to do a huge amount of catching up in terms of looking at architecture reading architecture going to exhibitions, I've started to use my pencil again a lot more and I feel like I'm in a happy place with that.

The notion of frustration as a result of unfulfiled creative ambitions is tackled by Helson (1999) and Helson and Pals (2000). Helson (1999) found that non-conformity is a positive and affirming trait in women for whom creative practice and work is really important to their sense of self. She explains that 'openness and unconventionality lead to creative productivity in a person for whom creative goals serve an integrative function' (p.99). However, for women who have a more complicated relationship with their creative side – for instance, who might have 'turned their back', as it were, on their creative talents – this unconventionality can be a contentious and painful thing, perhaps because they don't know how or where to channel those traits of running against the status quo. Helson and Pals (2000) use the categories of 'creative potential' and 'creative achievement' to test the theory that successfully constructing one's creative identity is necessary for ensuring that potential is transformed into achievement. They note that '(t) o order their work lives, individuals with creative potential must find an environment in which their identity as a person who engages in symbolic construction is supported' (p.5) but, as they point out, women have tended to have far fewer opportunities and been less likely to be facilitated in this than men. Since '(a) certain level of identity development is required to write a story that is recognized as original and beautiful, but the recognition received further confirms the individual's identity as a writer' (ibid.), it is critical that creative women would be supported in the construction of a creative identity.

It's suggested that, on the basis of Helson and Pals's (2000) paper on creative potential and creative achievement, the women comprising this study were found to have developed a strong creative identity and have, as a result, been successful at translating creative potential into creative achievement. Liz O'Kane talks about her work as a sculptor as not simply just 'work'. Instead it forms a very integral part of her identity, one which gives her a lot of pride: 'I eat, sleep, breathe what I do', she says. And she goes on, 'I love my work and I'm really proud of my work and if I'm in a new situation meeting new people, it does give me confidence to say I'm a sculptor and for most people that's quite interesting'. Una points to the importance of being open-minded and intelligent in order to create good work – the need to have a 'real interest in life and even talking to people and hearing their stories', as well as the openness to try new things throughout one's life. What is crucial also, she says, is that 'you have to be very self-motivated and to want to finish things as well'. This offers evidence of Una having developed a strong creative identity which has sustained her in her creative work.

On feeling a sense of pride in the work she does and how she identifies with it, Annie contends that her work is both a 'job' and also something more than that: 'it is my job, it's my career. It's very very important to me because without it I would be a very annoying person I would say'. This alludes to the integrative function of creative work for Annie in bringing together her creative potential with her creative identity, as per Helson and Pals (2000). Amanda Coogan expresses a similar sense that without being able to give expression to her creativity she 'wouldn't be a nice person'. Amanda's determination to make a living from performance art comes across very strongly in how she withstood pressure from her parents who wanted her to 'go and get a real job', especially when she could have made a very decent living from sign-language interpreting. She puts this down to the simple fact that she 'need[s] it'. In other words, being an artist is fundamental to her sense of self and identity and is a vital source of self-expression and satisfaction in her life.

> if I was a full-time lecturer in an art college or … if I had become a full-time mum, or if I was a full-time sign-language interpreter, I think that I'd be narky! I think I wouldn't be a nice person and I wouldn't be satisfied … And I always know if I'm doing too much interpreting, that I need to get back into the studio; that's the way I describe it, 'I need to get back into the studio'.

This chimes with Helson (1999) and Helson and Pals (2000) in highlighting the importance of creative output to women continuing in creative work. Amanda also exhibits a very established creative identity, something that Lelia Doolan also demonstrates. Lelia expresses having developed a creative identity through her association and work with others: 'You see I believe that creativity is not a single person's kind of insight, it's a gang that you kind of gather around you'. Furthermore, 'I'd feel that everyone is creative and that not a single artistic or creative act is without its cohort of co-inspirers and conspirators'. It's also a determination to find solutions to problems that arise, and she notes that 'being resilient I think is really important in being creative … And humour; humour, humour. If you do not have a fucking sense of humour, you may as well bury yourself now'. Lelia's sense of fun, her irreverence, and her insatiable energy for creative projects all form part of her creative identity. Considering that all of the women in this study exhibited solid creative identities and have been successful at ensuring that their creative potential is converted into creative achievement, one can argue that they all express a 'sense of harmony between self, art, and career' (Brooks and Daniluk, 1998, p.254), as Brooks and Daniluk found with their study cohort. They report that carving out a professional creative life for themselves 'enabled the women to experience a deep and satisfying sense of congruence between their sense of themselves and their work' (ibid.). Their creative achievements also provided 'meaning and purpose' as well as 'joy and pleasure' (p.254) for the women. This very much tracks with the place of creativity in the lives of the women interviewed for this study.

Perceptions of the labels 'artist' and 'creative'

While the women all showed themselves to have constructed strong creative identities, they reveal varying degrees of comfort with the labels of 'artist' and/or 'creative'. The different perceptions of what this label means or implies tend to be divided along generational lines, with Jess and Oonagh, as the youngest women interviewed for the study, expressing themselves as comfortable identifying as an 'artist' or 'creative', while most of the other women, older than these two, have a range of mostly similar misgivings that these terms bring to mind connotations of pretention or 'arty types' that feel too far away from their own personalities and approaches to work. In other words, these are stable, hardworking women, without the 'bohemian' or kind of self-destructive behaviours that they believe might typify or be stereotypical of 'creative'/artistic types.

On the question of identifying as an 'artist', Oonagh comments that she sees herself as a 'film artist', in part because she makes film and also because her projects get funding from the Arts Council. She credits the Arts Council with encouraging its recipients to take ownership of the word 'artist' and, for Oonagh, that reflects an encouragement to take the work 'seriously'. In addition, she says, 'I don't see "artist" as not meaning maternal or carer because I feel I took that on board as a word early enough in my career to feel like it could'. Jess, meanwhile, explains that in more recent years she views herself as 'more (of) a multifaceted person and that has allowed me to be more creative because my ego has been reduced'. She notes that

> It's been really freeing for me to see myself as someone who creates rather than someone who is a singer … my ego has less to hang onto and that's what you want … the more the ego is in the room the harder it is to be free with your creativity and free to play you know and that's really what creativity is, it's making make room within your life to play and that's why a lot of the time it's harder for women because it's harder for us to make room for ourselves to play, traditionally historically … it's not important for us as a society to have room for ourselves, it's important for us to contribute to families and to nurture and to support, to keep a home or to raise children and they were our roles and none of that has anything to do with us ever being alone to be with ourselves and to be with our own emotions and to process them to the point that they come out on paper or through music or through lyrics or through poetry or writing and so even that in itself is such a beautiful rebellion to take time and to make room for play.

This insight from Jess speaks to the discussion in the previous section in terms of the pressures on creative women in trying to manage and make room in their lives for family and children as well as their creative work. It also, in some respect, calls into question the myth or commonly understood perception of the artist as necessarily an isolated type of figure without any ties or social or family responsibilities. The focus on the artist as a 'solitary genius' is first seen around the 15th century with the publication of Alberti's text *On Painting* in 1435 (Chadwick, 1990). This is likely the first record that centres the artist as a person and their works as extensions of what they are trying to convey, rather than the situation prior to this, when the artwork itself is front and centre with the artist on the periphery. This emphasis on the artist as *auteur* is still at the heart of modern art criticism and art history scholarship. In this conceptualisation of the artist, as explored previously, women are generally excluded from assuming the identity label of artist since the works they give expression to are not considered worthy of much weight or value. In addition, women's occupying of other roles beyond 'artist' means they do not fit the mould of the solitary, genius creative type. Cultural depictions and representations of the artist-creative figure typically do not make room for women, especially women who are also mothers. Conor, Gill, and Taylor (2015) warn that 'images, representative figures and other depictions of a creative worker become a barrier to the recognition of particular categories of people, including women, as creative practitioners or professionals, perpetuating their exclusion and under-representation' (p.14). In other words, the image of the creative/artist that is present in the culture is mostly male, and the result is that society, creative industries and organisations, and women themselves struggle to square the figure of a woman with the labels 'creative' or 'artist'.

The difficulty in owning such labels is evident with some of this study's cohort. For instance, Lisa Mulcahy finds that 'artist' bears with it connotations of pretention and as such it offers a mould she feels she does not fit. She says,

> I would never say I am an artist ... because I could feel my brothers and sisters going 'what pretentiousness is that' so I would never regard myself as that but I suppose that is what I do, you know, of course that is what I do.

There is clearly some tension here in recognising that her work fits firmly within the artistic and creative sphere but actively claiming that label feels somehow not quite right. A similarly revealing exchange occurred with Annie, where she explained that she's also sceptical of the term 'artist' with its connotations of being 'terribly up yourself'. In other words, the supposed arrogance of the artist figure is something she loathes and something she doesn't see as representing herself and her own approach to creativity. Nevertheless, she contends that 'labels matter'. This is something of a contentious issue for illustrators since, as Annie describes it, they are the 'Cinderellas of the art world': forgotten, ignored, considered sell-outs, and undervalued in book publishing where all the credit goes to the author. Annie's attraction to design was, in part, because people working in this area were more down-to-earth. They were 'practical', 'solid', 'modest' people who 'got on with the job' and who lacked notions about their own importance. Liz references a related set of associated meanings with the label of 'artist'. She also finds it doesn't sit well with her, and equally so for sculptor friends of hers who find they don't subscribe to the term because of its connotations of 'dreamy', scruffy, 'scatty' types, whereas the reality, she explains, is that she and those she knows would be far more structured, focused, and hardworking than the general, public perception of an 'artist':

I think for a lot of non-artistic people they have that stereotype that artists are these real scatty people and people that mightn't start work until 12 in the afternoon or certainly don't get out of bed in the morning … so I think that society in general has maybe a derogatory image … of the term 'artist' whereas every single one of my artist friends and colleagues that I could name don't fall under that category; they would be really organised, successful, hardworking – really hardworking – people, who churn out really strong work that I respect and so are not these dreamy types who sit in cafés all day and smoke Gauloises cigarettes and dream about the next big success story or something; it's very much like any other job you just have to go in and put the time in and the work itself is quite solitary and you just get on with the work and then of course if there's an exhibition or an open night or an unveiling, they're the exciting times but mostly … there's a lot of drudgery in just day-to-day, normal work that you have to get through but that you enjoy anyway.

Una also suggests an understanding of the artist-type as 'hippy-dippy', as she puts it, something that clearly does not reflect her own personality or approach to life. Instead, she says she's more comfortable simply describing herself as 'graphic designer'. The distinction she suggests between those who call themselves artists-creatives and those who don't may be to do with the commercial aspects of a career like graphic design as opposed to 'fine art'. These allusions by Una, Annie, and Liz to the stereotypical conceptions of the artist as arrogant or self-important types versus the reality of the daily grind of artistic and creative work are important in calling for a cultural re-imagining of the artist figure. Abuhamdeh and Csikszentmihalyi (2004) similarly note the popular understanding of the artist as a difficult, tortured character and, in order to make their point, provide the example of the mental struggles Jackson Pollock endured. This characterisation is the antithesis of these women who, as previously described, are secure, emotionally healthy women who approach their work in a conscientious manner and who, as much as they may be unconventional and open-minded, do not embody 'hippy' traits or lifestyles.

The aspects of ego and self-absorption as stereotypical and necessary characteristics and qualities of the (male) artist are rejected by Marina Carr. Regarding her own self-perception or self-conceptualisation, when she peels away all the 'bullshit' and the trappings of identity, she really only considers herself a 'writer' during the actual act of writing. Similarly, she argues for the need to divorce the ego from the work and notes that it's not the role of the artist or writer to be a 'social commentator'. Instead, Marina says, the sole focus for the artist or writer is to create work that stands on its own, without the personality or personal viewpoints of the creator acting as a kind of currency in how the work is received.

Art and creative work that does not centre the creator but alternatively prioritises the work may better reflect, in general, women's approach to creativity. In any case, what is found in this study is that these creative women thoroughly enjoy and relish the act of creativity; work exceptionally hard to produce interesting, high quality, and skilled work; and take pride in the final output. The reluctance, on the part of some, to claim and own the labels of 'creative' and/or 'artist' is noteworthy but not of central importance. Nevertheless, this reluctance or difficulty is not unusual, with Brooks and Daniluk (1998) finding that their female creative interviewees also articulate a 'struggle to assume the identity of "artist"' (p.253). This resulted from a belief that they did not fit the mould of the 'artist' – a finding among this study's cohort – or that they hadn't acquired the 'requisite talent or credentials to legitimize their claims to be artists' (ibid.). The authors comment that the women resolve this dilemma at the time when they 'redefine' their understanding of what constitutes the figure of the artist. We see this process of negotiation in some comments made by Lisa, Annie, and Liz.

References

Abuhamdeh, S. and Csikszentmihalyi, M. (2004) 'The artistic personality: A systems perspective', in Sternberg, R.J., Grigorenko, E.L. and Singer, J.L. (eds.) *Creativity: From potential to realization.* Washington, DC: American Psychological Association, pp. 31–42.

Brooks, G.S. and Daniluk, J. C. (1998) 'Creative labors: The lives and careers of women artists', *The Career Development Quarterly*, 46(3), pp. 246–261. https://doi.org/10.1002/j.2161-0045.1998.tb00699.x.

Chadwick, W. (1990) *Women, art, and society.* London: Thames and Hudson.

Conor, B., Gill, R. and Taylor, S. (2015) 'Introduction: Gender and creative labour', in Conor, B., Gill, R. and Taylor, S. (eds.) *Gender and creative labour*. Chichester: Wiley-Blackwell, pp. 1–23.

Helson, R. (1999) 'A longitudinal study of creative personality in women', *Creativity Research Journal*, 12(2), pp. 89–101. https://doi.org/10.1207/s15326934crj 1202_2.

Helson, R. and Pals, J. L. (2000) 'Creative potential, creative achievement, and personal growth', *Journal of Personality*, 68(1), pp. 1–27. https://doi.org/10 .1111/1467-6494.00089.

Reis, S.M. (2002) 'Toward a theory of creativity in diverse creative women', *Creativity Research Journal*, 14(3–4), pp. 305–316. https://doi.org/10.1207/ S15326934CRJ1434_2.

6 Conclusions

Insights derived from creative women in Ireland

At the heart of this book are the arguments put forward in art historian Linda Nochlin's powerful 1971 essay 'Why Have There Been No Great Women Artists?' which suggests that the lack of encouragement, patronage, and support of women is to blame for their relative absence in creative and artistic endeavour; and in Carolyn Korsmeyer's hugely important work on *Gender and Aesthetics* (2004), which theorises and conceptualises how 'hidden gender', and in particular the higher value placed on the 'masculine' as opposed to the 'feminine' in dualistic understandings of the world, continues to greatly influence collective thinking on a range of issues – creative capability included. In addition, scholarship in the field of psychology and sociology with a focus on creativity has been essential in establishing that beliefs which maintain that women are less capable of creative work are in fact rooted more in biological determinism and gender essentialism and not in fact. Virginia Woolf, in a rejection of an essentialist view of women's abilities, wrote about the need for 'psychological androgyny' for anyone, of either sex, who strove to be creative. She references Coleridge to say that 'the androgynous mind is resonant and porous ... it transmits emotion without impediment ... it is naturally creative, incandescent and undivided' (Woolf, 1929, p.114).

In effect, the creative type, regardless of whether they're male or female, resists and rejects gender stereotypical behaviours, norms, and expectations. Some of the benefits of a psychological androgyny mentioned include 'cognitive flexibility, adaptability' and being 'less bound by gender-based stereotypes and expectations' (Keller, Lavish, and Brown, 2007, p.275), meaning such individuals have a greater catalogue of behaviour, emotional, and intellectual responses available with which to respond to creative work. Certainly the women who participated in this study show themselves to be adaptable, open-minded, and, while aware that the aspect of gender can impact the experiences and approach to creative work for women, largely not interested in the topic of gender nor overly concerned with sex-role

DOI: 10.4324/9781003082750-6

norms and expectations. Consequently, they exhibit androgynous traits in the sense of 'incorporating' (see Wolff and Taylor, 1979 for further on this) behaviours and approaches to their life and creative work that could be considered stereotypical to both sexes. In other words, the women in this study were warm, compassionate, relational, and caring, all qualities typically associated with women. But they were also very driven, determined, tenacious, and highly creative, which are characteristics more commonly considered masculine and thereby linked with men.

Turning attention from the fields of philosophy and psychology to the sociological, Conor, Gill, and Taylor (2015) echo Nochlin's insight more than 40 years later by noting that the relative lack of women, particularly in creative roles, across the CCIs is not helped by a networking approach to hiring, which sees men propose other males for vacant positions. This reality, however, is obscured by a culture of individual self-promotion that accompanies such work and an assertion that passion alone and a will to 'Do What You Love' (p. 2) is all that is required to succeed in the creative space. On that basis, if women are not securing creative work, it's a negative reflection on their desire and drive to be involved in these industries. This emphasis on self-promotion and constructing a 'brand' for oneself is more contentious for women than men, given the mythic recognition of the creative worker as being male. That creativity is socially and culturally understood to be a male trait (Nixon, 2003; Windels and Lee, 2012; Hesmondhalgh and Baker, 2015) not only has a potentially massive impact on the content emanating from the art and culture industries, but as Hesmondhalgh and Baker (2015) point out, there is also a degree of esteem and status implicit in creative roles that is thereby mostly only afforded to male creative practitioners. In addition to assumptions of women's competence lying in the direction of communication and caring skills, the authors identify another unhelpful supposition in the realm of the cultural industries: the belief that women are better organisers and logisticians than men. This impacts female creatives since such skills are thought to be in direct contrast to those needed for creative work. Although the women interviewed for this study mostly work for themselves or in a freelance capacity and therefore don't face these issues of organisational bias in favour of men, they did face some challenges during their professional years that resulted from sexism, discrimination, and gender bias. While these experiences were discouraging, they were not overly so, with the women displaying a resilience and grit to not be beaten down by such incidents.

Engaging with scholarship in the above areas, this work has sought to offer the perspective and insight of creative women who challenge the engrained misconceptions of creativity as a fundamentally male capacity. It contributes to the feminist project of objecting to sweeping essentialist and neurosexist contentions of male and female 'brains', aptitudes, and suitability to certain kinds of – especially 'high' and transcendent – work and endeavours by foregrounding both debates and examples that undermine the gendered construction of the artist-creator as male. Centuries of theorising and discourse about the source and nature of creativity have brought us to a place where, in our collective subconscious, 'women are associated with *pro*creativity' (Korsmeyer, 2004, p.14; emphasis in original) and men with creativity. This 'biology is destiny' or gender essentialist worldview continues to resonate and dominate in artistic and creative fields. The research that has underpinned this book set out to treat the women featured as individuals, each with her own rich inner creative life and whose insights would offer a valuable counter perspective to the belief that women cannot transcend their biology in order to achieve creative heights.

In the tradition of critical theory, what is at stake in any scholarly work underpinned by feminist considerations and principles is a concern for the real-world and material experience of being female. In other words, whether it is predominately philosophical and theoretical, or whether it is rooted in a sociological examination of industries and structures, or whether the work is ethnographically grounded in the sense and meaning that research subjects make from their culture and their experiences, feminist research retains at its core a commitment to bringing about some change for the betterment of women and girls. As bell hooks put it,

> Feminist focus on finding a voice may sound clichéd at times … However, for women within oppressed groups … coming to voice is an act of resistance. Speaking becomes both a way to engage in active self-transformation and a rite of passage where one moves from being object to being subject. Only as subjects can we speak.
>
> (cited in Storey, 2009, p.136)

This assertion by hooks offers a reminder of how crucial it is in terms of meanings and identity that we as women contribute our own stories to the cultural and artistic canon without assuming there is one homogenous 'experience' shared by all women. Nevertheless, what we do share is the experience of being female in patriarchal societies.

Building on the influential work of feminist scholars examining and critiquing our symbolic world, this study has aimed to make a contribution to their insights into the nature and impact of the patriarchal concept of gender on our cultural sphere by drawing together the various strands of philosophy, psychology, and cultural sociology, with the addition of the crucial component of hearing directly from creative women about the role and importance of creativity to their lives. As Millett so astutely wrote in

1970, '(w)hatever the "real" differences between the sexes may be, we are not likely to know them until the sexes are treated differently, that is alike. And this is very far from being the case at present' (p.39). This research is predicated on that call to action of treating the sexes alike – or, to be more accurate, of treating women like human beings, of assuming women to be a diverse, multidimensional, multifaceted group driven by disparate interests and motivations, a courtesy and assumption long extended to men and to male creatives. Consequently, this book has sought to elevate the work undertaken by fellow scholars by offering illustrative and informative examples of the abundance of creativity residing in many women.

What remains to be said is to consider how to best support and nurture creativity in girls and women. As the findings of this study indicate, the three areas of home, education, and industry or the professional sphere are where attention is needed. In the home environment, it is clear, from the conducive environments that most of this study's cohort grew up in, that girls need significant levels of freedom – both in a tangible, physical sense as well as psychologically – in order for them to be able to explore their nascent creativity. The experience of having a secure and loving family but one where there is a kind of 'benign' disinterest or indifference on the part of parents to their daughters' creative interests is a positive one. Having said that, every woman in this study references someone in their early lives who offered encouragement by ensuring that, as girls, they understood that they had some creative talent. Often such encouragement is provided by teachers in primary school. This speaks to the importance of the educational realm in terms of facilitating and supporting girls in their creativity. The women interviewed describe, at secondary school but also into higher education, relationships with key figures such as teachers, lecturers, tutors, and mentors who showed faith in them and provided space for them to learn and grow by taking a chance on them.

For the educational sector, especially in terms of thinking about courses that teach and train creative practitioners, there must be greater recognition of the role of encouragement and mentorship in fostering the talents of girls and women. Given that research has shown that social and external factors can negatively impact on girl's creativity (Thomas and Berk, 1981; Reis, 2002) and experiences in school and university, this can be detrimental to the creative confidence of girls and young women. And while there's no 'one size fits all' approach to nurturing creativity in girls and, as Reis (2002) notes, '(t)he development of a creative life is intricate and complex' (p.315), it is paramount that teachers and tutors are aware of these biases and would seek to mitigate them. This could involve designing courses and curricula to ensure that female students are mentored by established women in their chosen creative field, in addition to, for example, ensuring equal numbers of male and female creators of film, music, art, literature, and so forth when choosing works and practitioners for students to engage with on a curriculum. For young women to be mentored by and to be exposed to the creative works of other women is critical for enabling them to understand the breadth of female creative talent, as well as to develop a sense of female creative legacy so that girls and women can see a path for themselves and not feel that they have to continuously 'reinvent the wheel' or feel that they must be pioneers in carving out unchartered territory.

The third and final area that requires immediate attention is in the professional space. In particular, the findings of this study highlight the challenges that women who are mothers face in trying to manage both their creative work and the demands of motherhood. While it goes without saying that the women interviewed who have children cherish their experience of motherhood and even if they would not do anything differently – especially in terms of, in some instances, taking a step back in their creative professions in order to devote more time to their children – it's clear that the reasons they could continue in their chosen creative fields was, in part, because of the aspect of having very involved and supportive husbands, partners, and fathers. Nevertheless, the women would have benefited from more supports. This is particularly the case for those women more attached to established industries, such as architecture and the film and television industries. Not surprisingly, the aspects of childcare and flexible working arrangements are crucial for enabling women in the creative industries to sustain their careers after having children. As such, initiatives like Raising Films, which was originally set up in the UK and now has a presence in Ireland, was established to 'start a conversation about being a parent, carer and a filmmaker' (Wreyford, O'Brien, and Dent, 2021, p.60) and to seek to create change in the film industry by normalising this fact. The unique challenges that mothers must overcome when working in the creative sphere necessitate strong support networks. In Ireland, groups like MAM (Mothers Artists Makers), whose Twitter account, @MamIreland, describes itself as 'a feminist movement created by mothers who are professional members of the creative industries', offer such support. This group and the findings of this study highlight the fact that creative women who are mothers are not lacking in motivation or hunger. Rather, the reality of their continued creative involvement puts paid to assertions that mothers do not make good creatives.

There is much that is very hopeful to take away from the findings of this study. The women interviewed wonderfully articulated the joy, fulfilment, and satisfaction they glean from their creative work. They talk about their involvement in creativity in ways that suggest it constituted a 'need' rather than it being simply a professional choice. In other words, the role of creativity in their lives is such that it provides important outlets for self-expression and forms an integral part of their identity. This relationship to creativity proves critical in terms of successfully converting 'creative potential' into 'creative achievement'. And while it has not, in any way, stunted their creative productivity, where there is some 'room for improvement', so to say, is with respect to their perception of what it means to label oneself a 'creative' or 'artist'. For the most part, the women tend to reject self-describing themselves in such ways since they made associations between these labels and a figure in whom they don't see themselves reflected. This points to the need, in our culture and in our societies, of more diverse archetypes of the creative. For a start, there should be far more examples of women represented as embodying this figure. If this is achieved, girls and boys growing up would no longer make assumptions about the creative-artist figure as male and instead would conceive of creativity as simply a human trait, skill, drive, and endeavour.

References

Conor, B., Gill, R. and Taylor, S. (2015) 'Introduction: Gender and creative labour', in Conor, B., Gill, R. and Taylor, S. (eds.) *Gender and creative labour*. Chichester: Wiley-Blackwell, pp. 1–23.

Hesmondhalgh, D. and Baker, S. (2015) 'Sex, gender and work segregation in the cultural industries', in Conor, B., Gill, R. and Taylor, S. (eds.) *Gender and creative labour*. Chichester: Wiley-Blackwell, pp. 23–36.

Keller, C.J., Lavish, L.A. and Brown, C. (2007) 'Creative styles and gender roles in undergraduate students', *Creativity Research Journal*, 19(2–3), pp. 273–280.

Korsmeyer, C. (2004) *Gender and aesthetics: An introduction*. New York: Routledge.

Millett, K. (1970) *Sexual politics*. Champaign, IL: University of Illinois Press.

Nixon, S. (2003) *Advertising cultures: Gender, commerce, creativity*. London and Thousand Oaks, CA: SAGE.

Nochlin, L. (1971) 'Why have there been no great women artists?' in Baker, E. and Hess, T.B. (eds.) *Art and sexual politics*. New York: Macmillan, pp. 194–205.

Reis, S.M. (2002) 'Toward a theory of creativity in diverse creative women', *Creativity Research Journal*, 14(3–4), pp. 305–316. https://doi.org/10.1207/S15326934CRJ1434_2.

Storey, J. (2009) *Cultural theory and popular culture: An introduction* (5th ed.). Boca Raton, FL: Routledge.

Thomas, N.G. and Berk, L.E. (1981) 'Effects of school environments on the development of young children's creativity', *Child Development*, 52(4), pp. 1153–1162. https://doi.org/10.2307/1129501.

Windels, K. and Lee, W.N. (2012) 'The construction of gender and creativity in advertising creative departments', *Gender in Management: An International Journal*, 27(8), pp. 502–519.

Wolff, L. and Taylor, S.E. (1979) 'Sex, sex-role identification, and awareness of sex-role stereotypes', *Journal of Personality*, 47(1), pp. 177–184. https://doi.org/10.1111/j.1467-6494.1979.tb00621.x.

Woolf, V. (1929) *A room of one's own*. London: Hogarth Press.

Wreyford, N., O'Brien, D. and Dent, T. (2021) 'Creative majority: An APPG for creative diversity report on 'what works' to support, encourage and improve diversity, equity and inclusion in the creative sector', *A report for the all party parliamentary group for creative diversity*. Available at: http://www.kcl.ac.uk/cultural/projects/creative-majority (Accessed: 4 April 2022).

Index

For Product Safety Concerns and Information please contact our EU
representative GPSR@taylorandfrancis.com
Taylor & Francis Verlag GmbH, Kaufingerstraße 24, 80331 München, Germany

www.ingramcontent.com/pod-product-compliance
Lightning Source LLC
Chambersburg PA
CBHW050537270326
41926CB00015B/3277